Flower arrangement week by week

KATINKA HENDRICHS

FLOWER ARRANGEMENT WEEK BY WEEK

WITH
60 ARRANGEMENTS
BY
JET KUYVENHOVEN

LUTTERWORTH PRESS•LONDON

First published in Great Britain 1970
Second Impression 1971

Copyright © 1969 Zomer & Keuning, Wageningen, Holland
English translation copyright © 1970 by Lutterworth Press

PHOTOGRAPHS: JAN DE HENGST
Translation by B. K. Bowes

ISBN 0 7188 1708 7

Printed in the Netherlands

Contents

Introduction   9

Containers   11

Holding equipment   13

The flowers   20

60 flowers arrangements in colour: 23

January   *Winter white*   24
          Sunny colours in the cold   26
          Tulips and marbles   28
          The first shrubs are in bloom   30

February *Spring indoors*   32
          A heart for St. Valentine   34
          Out of the cold, into the warm   36
          Narcissi   38

March   *Hothouse flowers*   40
          From garden and hothouse   42
          Subtle play with twigs   44
          Begin the spring gaily   46
          A mixed basket   48

April   *Easter egg*   50
          A tower for a table   52
          Blue and blue   54
          An arrangement of blossom   56

May   *Rhododendrons and guelder roses*   58
          May flowers   60
          Lilies-of-the-valley   62
          Flowers in a basin   64
          Lilac and pink   66

June	*A grid full of early plants*	68
	One arrangement, three containers	70
	A bowl of flowers	72
	Warm as the summer	74
	A gift in a glass	76
July	*Variation on the arrangement of wild flowers*	78
	Summer colours in a teapot	80
	Quiet yellow to loud orange	82
	Blue with and without prickles	84
August	*From the grass verges*	86
	All in white	88
	Cheap and dear go well together	90
	Two flowers in one colour	92
	Sunflowers	94
September	*Dahlias in a flat-iron*	96
	Late roses	98
	The autumn is coming	100
	Contrast composition	102
October	*Autumn harvest*	104
	Berries in a bottle	106
	Subtle autumn	108
	Arrangement of berries	110
	All in orange	112
November	*The last leaves from outside*	114
	Simple piece	116
	Old tints in new flowers	118
	From the tropics	120
December	*Mingled coppers*	122
	New ideas	124
	Start the winter like this	126
	Christmas begins at the front door	128
	Christmas ball	130
	A Christmas decoration on a shelf	132
	Gold for the Christmas table	134

A special everlasting arrangement   136
Dry in summer, enjoy in winter   138
Flowers from the world   140
A corsage for a dress or bracelet   142

Index   144

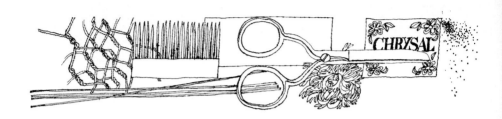

Introduction

Arise, my heart, go forth and seek,
In this beloved summertime,
In God's gifts your delight;
For you and me He glorifies
The gardens spread before our eyes,
With riches all bedight.
Paul Gerhardt

Touching flowers gives us a daily returning, delighted wonder over the many thousands of forms and colours in which they display their beauty. Snowdrops and witch hazel catkins appear very early on as a reward for our tense anticipation, as the first signs of life of the new year. There is a subtle pleasure in making a small arrangement with snowdrops supported by some leaves from evergreen bushes. Handling the delicate flowers and arranging them according to our own taste and ideas is an experience quite different from admiring flowers in gardens or fields from a distance.

Every month, every week and every day of the whole year can give us the pleasure of flowers in many different moods: festally exuberant, sweet and tender, or glowing and warm. It may be a sturdy arrangement of proud tulips, or a friendly blue dish of forget-me-nots. Sometimes we shall have a dashing but delicately coloured group; another week will see a charming nosegay of lilies of the valley with their quiet fragrance. In summer, abundant armfuls will let rooms and kitchens share in our joy over the flowering garden and the waving wild flowers of the roadside. Autumn will live on indoors, with berries and hips, with warm-tinted chrysanthemums; and anything that is grown and raised in hothouses will give us the warmth of a colourful, fragrant flower arrangement throughout the year, even when all is frost and snow or hail and storms out of doors.

If you have never tried to arrange flowers you may be stimulated by this book into pleasant adventures, in imitation of the arrangements described, free interpretations, or new inventions according to your own fancy and taste. You may discover a new dimension, which is there for everybody and is only waiting to be enjoyed with the eye and heart.

Containers

The really enthusiastic arranger will have discovered long ago that you can never have too many containers. At the outset about five of different sizes will seem to be a pretty good collection. But as you advance, using an ever-increasing variety of flowers, you will discover more and more that twenty, of different sizes, materials and colours, are by no means too many.

In spring and summer, when there are plenty of flowers in your own garden and flowers can be bought at a reasonable price, you will need wide and tall containers, to make expansive displays. Jugs, tall kettles, large glass goblets, milk cans, baskets or little casks will then be needed.

Do not hesitate to use baskets or wooden containers. Line them wih a thick layer of plastic or aluminium foil, and fill them with holding blocks (Oasis, Mossette or Florapak) cut to size, sphagnum, green twigs or a combination of these materials, or put a tin container inside them. The top of the latter should always be an inch or so below the edge of the basket or cask and therefore out of sight. You will then have an excellent basis for a tall, wide-spreading arrangement. In early spring, when a trip to the orchard, which is usually pruned in February, may provide you with a load of cherry, apple or pear branches, one of these large containers will come in very handy. They will certainly be useful when the thick sticky buds of the chestnut are ready to open in the warm room and the handsome hairy fingers spread out; and we have a long enjoyment of a big arrangement of blossoming sprays, bought when in bud or cut from the tree! The useful malus and prunus species will combine excellently with mainly ornamental varieties. First, we have the bold line of the brown wood, studded with little buds. Then comes the gradually increasing pleasure of watching them swell; at last they burst into a green haze. Finally, our happiness is completed by the white and pink flowers. You simply must have a tall, handsome container for an arrangement of this sort, which gives at least three weeks of enjoyment.

In spring, late autumn and winter, however, flowers are scarce, expensive and sometimes short-stemmed; medium-sized containers then come into their own. Small jugs, goblets and dishes with stems (these make an arrangement of short flowers seem much higher), bottles and carafes may be used to produce a

Here is some of this arranger's collection of containers for flowers: glasses on stems, big and little, two very different kettles, a homely thick earthenware crock and jug, an old white water jug, a soup tureen, a flat tray, a very smart covered butterdish, a sauce-boat, and a huge "vase": a bricklayer's bucket, rusty and battered.

11

striking arrangement with only a few flowers.

Then we have the time of very small, delicate flowers: snowdrops, scillas and violets, and later on sweet peas, buttercups and ragged robins. Elegant little pots are needed for these, perhaps a pretty cream pot that you have removed from your dressing table and put on the container shelf. Or you could try using comic stone mustard pots with inscriptions on them, or a milk jug from an old tea service, or one of those tiny cream jugs for serving cream in restaurants. Do not forget how your children seize every opportunity to pick flowers for you along the verges and in meadows. Notice how short they leave the stalks, and make sure that even those little bunches, given to you with so much love, are shown to full advantage. Shallow, straight pots or glasses are ideal for these short-stemmed but often bulging bunches.

Learn to inspect with a critical eye all the bottles and pots in which you buy food. There are some pretty mayonnaise bottles (Kraft), pot-bellied, narrow-necked bottles for some sorts of vinegar, mustard pots in a thousand and one sizes, pretty, glass ginger jars, fat glass jam jars and handsome white earthenware marmalade pots with inscriptions fired on them, to name only a few. If you have a good look round, you will find many more attractive pots and bottles of different brands. At least one specimen of all the kinds that you like should be kept on the container shelf in a cupboard or cellar.

Bowls, low dishes or bowls on stands also belong on this shelf. For these may be made suitable for flower arrangements as well as for the potting of bulbs blooming in the spring, such as paperwhites, hyacinths and tulips, by means of a piece of holding material cut to size, a pin-holder or a lump of sphagnum secured with wire.

Even a well-shaped piece of log may be suitable. Cut a hole in the heart for the holding equipment, using a sharp knife or a chisel, and make it water-tight if necessary with a few layers of nail varnish or paraffin wax; fortunately, the holding material retains a great deal of water. You now have an excellent container for a spring arrangement; for example a few cut flowers and twigs with a flowering hyacinth, or an autumn arrangement including one or two toadstools.

A good mixed collection of containers made up of those elements will satisfy you again each week, when you find that you have a suitable holder for each kind of flower; not to mention birthdays and other festive occasions, when visitors turn up with yet another bunch, for which you have the right vase, jug, bottle or bowl.

Holding equipment

Pin-holders

There are many sorts of pin-holder on the market. They are certainly not an ideal solution for every problem; soft stems are ruined, and thin stems do not get enough support; but they do make things easy for the beginner, though goes against the grain to press soft stems hard onto the sharp points.

Nevertheless, woody stems will absorb water better through these frayed holes, and this is justifiable, since woody stems are often beaten with a hammer until they are soft before being used in an arrangement.

When buying a pin-holder, make sure that it is heavy enough, in other words cast in lead, and that the pins are made of copper. Never buy painted pin-holders. The coat of paint will disappear very quickly under water, and then rusting metal pins will appear; rust is very harmful to flowers. If necessary, you can make your own pin-holder. Drive a large number of small copper nails through the underside of a tin lid, and then fill the lid with well made-up cement. This kind will not last for years, but it is useful; moreover, you can make it as big as you like, which is very welcome in view of the high prices of the large pin-holders in the shops.

If you are using light flowers, the weight of the lid is usually enough to prevent your arrangement from toppling over, but if branches and heavier flowers are used, the pin-holder should be anchored. Dry the dish and pin-holder very carefully; knead a piece of modelling clay or plasticine until it is soft, put it in the bottom of the pot, and press the pin-holder into it. If the pin-holder is going to show it must be concealed. First, wind some green adhesive tape, insulating tape or special green flower tape round the edge to hide the pins from the side. Pieces of moss, gravel, marble chips or even marbles may also be used to cover up the pin-holder where it is visible. For arrangements on a low dish, one or two flowers or leaves may be inserted very near the bottom, so as to hide the pins from view.

Plastic balls with holes in them and a suction cup on the underside are on sale for arrangements of light flowers. Similar balls, without suction cups and made of earthenware, are obtainable; sometimes they fit a goblet or bowl on a stem. These aids are very useful for making a spherical arrangement. Generally speaking, however, they tie you down too much to the shape, the positions of the holes and the need to follow this shape exactly so that the whole of the pin-holder is invisible.

Chicken wire

Chicken wire is an ideal solution for very many flower-holding problems. Choose a flexible type of fine wire, which can easily be pressed into shape. If you use wire with a fairly small mesh (see photograph on page 15), then you can generally manage with a piece that is about twice as long as the height of your container and somewhat wider. Fold it double in a rough curve, crumple it, and fit this wad in the container so that the wire is about three quarters of an inch below the edge and therefore invisible. If you choose fine wire with one-inch large meshes or so, then you should always make sure that five layers can be pressed into the container zigzag fashion.

There is plastic-coated wire: this is generally more difficult to bend and push into the right size, but it may be useful in silver containers, because ordinary chicken wire may cause discoloration, and this plastic-coated wire will naturally scratch the silver less. The same applies to a valuable crystal vase.

Now that we are on the subject of glass and crystal vases, I need not point out that the use of aids is usually troublesome. A large pin-holder at the bottom is ugly, a wad of chicken wire is too clearly visible if a fairly small number of flowers are used, and a great deal of green filling will rob the vase of its transparent charm. The best thing to do is to cut a piece of small-mesh chicken wire, which is a half or three quarters of an inch larger than the opening of the container and secure it firmly round the edge with fine wire. A few flowers, leaves or twigs put in near the bottom will conceal the chicken wire. You can use the same method for covering low dishes.

Never use your flower secateurs for cutting your chicken wire to size; these must remain sharp. Use special metal snips, kitchen scissors or an old ordinary pair specially reserved for the purpose.

Holding blocks

There are three brands of plastic holding material on the market: Oasis, Mossette and Florapak. Some must be crumbled or kneaded, while others merely need to be cut to the right size and used as blocks. But they must all be thoroughly soaked in water before use. It is best to place the block or kneaded lump in a bucket of warm water until it sinks like a stone. Only then can you be sure that it is thoroughly wet, and that the centre has not remained dry. If it is dry,

Wire netting, which may be used folded into a wad inside a container, or stretched over the top as a support. Three pinholders, and a reel of green flower tape, which is used to help conceal a pin-holder if necessary, and to reinforce weak stems. A sharp knife and secateurs to cut stalks and branches and for pruning: and (below) a pair of cutters for wire netting.

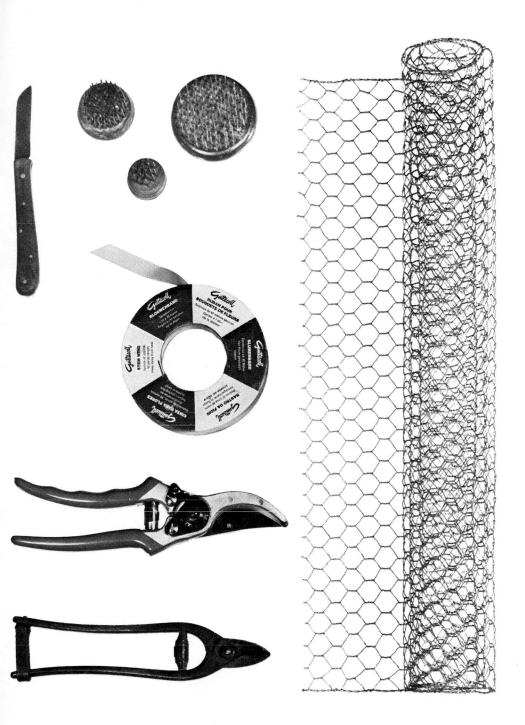

flowers will wilt in no time at all.

If you are using a vase, just make sure it is filled to an inch or two below the edge; but if you are using a dish, you can prevent the block or kneaded lump from falling apart by cutting it to the right size, wrapping it in a piece of chicken wire and securing it to the edge of the dish with wire.

With a vase, you may use for cheapness a combination of greenery and holding material. Place conifer twigs inside the vase upside down, round the edge; fill the centre with a holding block or a piece of one.

This material is expensive for daily use, but it is very succesful for making special, difficult arrangements. It can be employed without a container, for example for making a wall decoration or an arrangement for a cupboard shelf (see page 132), an Easter egg (see page 50) or a heart for Saint Valentine's Day (see page 34). For extra stiffening, you may pack the block in chicken wire after you have cut it to size, or else wind string or fine wire round it. If it is going to be placed against a wall, on the edge of a mirror frame or on a shelf, then you should stick a piece of wood, hardboard, thick aluminium foil folded double or thick plastic on the underside, to prevent penetration by damp. For dried-flower arrangements, you will naturally use dry holding material.

Sphagnum

Most florists can supply sphagnum. A box of this, stored and kept damp in your flower-arranging corner or in the cellar, will be of inestimable service for arrangements in boxes and dishes. It is much cheaper than the various types of artificial holding material. It is not a difficult material to use, although a little more patience and dedication is needed.

For a dish, take a good piece of sphagnum, give it the desired shape, wind string or wire round the ball, oblong piece or square block, and secure it to the edge of the dish with wire. Balls of sphagnum are also very attractive in baskets (lined with plastic or aluminium foil) or on pieces of hardboard cut to size (see the Saint Valentine's Day heart on page 34) and for decorating tables, cupboards or mirrors.

Foam plastic holding material, sold in various sizes under the names Oasis (shown here), Florapak and Mossette. Sphagnum moss (left middle) is very reliable as a basis for "free" arrangements with no container, on say a mirror frame or a lacquer tray. (Right) conifer twigs are invaluable for holding arrangements in large containers. (Below and at right) green wire, flower binding wire, in different thicknesses is used to support or lengthen stems where necessary, and to fix the different sorts of holding material in position.

Even a Christmas decoration or Easter egg (see pages 130 and 50) may be made of sphagnum. It may be used alone for an Easter egg that is not too large; for a large Easter egg or Christmas decoration, pinch some chicken wire into the correct shape, and drape round it a thick layer of sphagnum, which should be fixed by winding string or wire round it. Short-stemmed flowers, twigs and berries are used, of course, because long stems do not find any water in the hollow ball. For Christmas decorations using a great deal of holly, fir twigs, fir cones and Iceland moss, this does not present much difficulty, and naturally does not matter at all with dried flowers. But if thirsty cut flowers are used, the problem must be borne in mind. For Easter eggs, a holding block may be combined with sphagnum. Use the block, well saturated with water, as a core, wind the sphagnum round it in the shape of an egg, and fix it with string or wire. This has the advantage that any sphagnum visible between the flowers and leaves will look much more natural than a foam-plastic holder.

Both artificial, foam-plastic holding blocks and sphagnum must, of course, have a good long damping every other day with a spray or a watering-can. The ball or lump should be held over the kitchen sink to allow surplus water to run off. Alternatively, if the nature of the flowers permits, dip it in a bucket of water.

Gravel and marbles

Gravel, marble chips and marbles are indispensable aids to flower arrangement, particularly if you use flat dishes a great deal. Gravel is ideal to conceal the holding block, sphagnum or pin-holder. Gravel and marbles are also very useful with glass vases or tanks. Some flower shops and interior-decoration shops sell colourless or plain tinted glass balls specially for use as flower supports. If you cannot get hold of these, then a dip in your children's marbles bag may be profitable. But the colour of the marbles must harmonize as far as possible with the colours of the flower arrangement. A glass tank or vase filled with quite heavy glass balls, marbles or gravel is not, of course, suitable for flowers with delicate stems such as sweet peas or wild poppies. But flowers with stiff stems, for example roses and irises, tulips, delphiniums, African marigolds or sturdy Oriental poppies can be inserted fairly easily. A base of this kind is also naturally suitable for all kinds of branches carrying blossoms or leaves.

Greenery

Conifers are generally used for greenery. If you think it is a pity to keep sacrificing the twigs of your garden conifers, then ask your florist for this material. He has plenty of it and will let you have it at a reasonable price. Conifer greenery keeps well for a very long time and can be kept in a bucket with some water in it. If you rinse it very carefully after use, trim it again, remove rotting parts and see that it does not smell, you can use it several times.

Cut branches of greenery that are about as long as the vase or tank is high. Place them in the vase upside down. The flower stems are then more easily inserted downwards past the spiky leaves than "against the grain". The ends should project about three quarters of an inch above the edge of the vase. Two strong pieces of binding wire should then be pushed through them crosswise and wound round the edge of the vase or bowl. This will prevent the greenery from falling away when you start arranging, and it is not visible when you have finished.

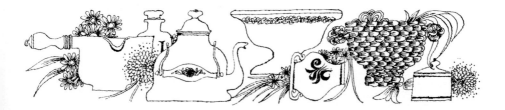

The flowers

Stiffening the stems

It is generally best to arrange the different kinds of flowers in natural positions; the stems should not be forced to bend unnaturally by means of binding wire. Tulips are an exception. They behave obstinately in the container, often continuing to grow and standing up proudly after a time. They may therefore upset a subtle balance or destroy the line of a careful arrangement of a few flowers. Tulip stems can be fixed with green binding wire in one of two ways. Push the wire into the stem an inch or two below the flower, form it into a loop, and then wind it downwards along and as close as possible to the stem. Alternatively, push the wire into the centre of the flower, and wind it downwards along and close to the stem. According to a third method, the wire may be pushed into the flower and then held close to and along the stem. Green flower tape may then be wound round the two. This may cause less breaking; there is a knack in winding wire downwards along the stem, and you are sure to break one or two at first. But the glossy green plastic stem is certainly not attractive or natural. If you are very accurate and patient, you can push wire through the stem from the bottom; this is quite easy with narcissi and zinnias, but rather more difficult with tulips.

Roses may soon show a tendency to droop, especially if they are bought in a shop. You can support them by pushing binding wire through the bottom of the flower and passing it down along the stem. To prevent the weary and often top-heavy heads of chrysanthemums and zinnias from drooping, push a toothpick, pointed match or cocktail stick straight through the heart of the flower and into the stem so that the wood projects no further than the stamens in the heart. Stems supported by wire can be gently bent into the desired form. The same applies to woody branches. These can be bent to some extent without wire, but gently. The part to be bent is held firmly with all the fingers of both hands. The curve is stroked long and carefully with the thumbs, the branch being bent more and more (taking care, of course, that it does not break) until the desired position is reached and the wood no longer springs back.

To lengthen short stems that must come high up in the arrangement, you may lay a piece of stem or thick wire along the bottom four inches of the branch or flower to be used, and attach the two to each other with green flower tape or green binding wire. The flower stem or branch must, of course, already be long enough to stand in the water of the container. The extra piece of stem is only for fixing the flower or branch more easily in the desired position; this is difficult if the stem is only just in the container.

Before you start arranging
The best time to pick flowers in the garden is generally in the early morning or evening after sunset. A large flat flower-basket is ideal; the flowers are not bruised so quickly. If they are picked during fierce sunshine they will very soon wilt. But if you must or wish to pick them in the daytime, always take a bucket of water outside with you, put it in a shady place and place the picked flowers in it as soon as possible.

Before you use bought flowers, wrap them in paper and put them in fresh water for about an hour, preferably in a cool, dark place, so that the limp stems become stiff again after their journey. The dried ends of the stem should be cut back a little with a sharp knife or sharp secateurs, preferably with a slanting cut, so as to increase the suction surface.

Take a large wad of cotton wool, an old newspaper and a large plastic bag with you for picking flowers in the country. Dip the cotton wool in water (you will always find a ditch or puddle), and wrap the ends of the stems in it. Pack the bunch loosely in newspaper, and put this into the plastic bag. Inflate the bag, and close it well by knotting it or using a piece of string. Inflating reduces the risk of staining the flowers. This is also an ideal way of carrying a bunch of flowers to give as a present, or conveying a corsage from home to a party or wedding. Never put flowers in ice-cold water. The shock of this cold foot-bath is certainly bad for flowers picked in a hot summer garden.

Some people treat woody stems with boiling water. This has the same preservative effect as scorching. Take a sharp knife, and cut obliquely to the desired length the branches with their flowers or leaves, including roses. Than tap a length of about two inches gently with a hammer, so that the branch becomes fibrous. Immediately afterwards, scorch it in a candle flame or plunge it in boiling water as deep as possible, as far as the leaf or flower. The branches should stay in the water until it has cooled. The flowers or leaves should be protected from the steam by packing in blotting paper.

If you do not like the idea of scorching or dipping in boiling water, cut and tap the woody stems, and put the flowers in lukewarm water straight away. If roses should nod their heads, you can persuade them to hold them up again proudly by cutting their stems obliquely under water, removing as many leaves as possible, wrapping the flowers firmly in paper and then placing the stems in warm water for a few hours.

You *must* scorch stems with a great deal of milky juice, such as spurge or poinsettia (*Euphorbia pulcherrima*) and poppies. Cut them obliquely to the desired length, and hold the cut end over a candle flame. Then they are ready for your arrangement.

Mimosa sprays with their tiny fragrant yellow globes, those friendly harbingers of spring from the south, must be put in hot water. And if possible use the special yellow mimosa Chrysal.

There are various ways of keeping the water in your containers clean. Some put in a piece of charcoal, which keeps the water clear. Others add a drop of bleaching fluid to achieve the same effect. A spoonful of sugar or an aspirin are good food, but the easiest method is the special cut-flower food, Chrysal.

Sixty flower arrangements in colour

Winter white

The container: Glass bowls on a tall stem are excellent for short-stemmed flowers and enable them to be used for an arrangement that can be placed somewhere other than the well-known low table in the middle of the sitting-room. A very small arrangement will usually be out of place on a sideboard or cupboard, but one of these arrangements will be just right there.

The holding material: For this kind of bowl, cut to size or knead a piece of Oasis or some other holding material, soak it thoroughly, and secure it round the edge of the bowl with wire pushed through crosswise. Or use a ball of sphagnum. Whichever you choose, make sure that the material is wet right to the heart, so that each flower can absorb water properly.

The arrangement: When the holly is taken down after Christmas, the house looks very bare, and we have a long time to wait until spring. Nothing is then more delightful than to indulge in a bunch of spring flowers, for example paperwhites with their wonderful perfume. As you no doubt know, these are a kind of narcissus, which you can quite easily bring into flower from the bulbs on pebbles or marble chips. Their delicate loose tufts of flower can be combined in a beautiful white arrangement with white roses (those in the picture are sold under the name Tiara), white dried everlasting flowers (in this case, we used the large-flowered double *Helichrysum bracteatum monstrosum flore pleno var. snowball*) and green and white leaves, for example variegated ivy. There are various kinds of this ivy for the garden, for example *Hedera helix var. argente ovarieagata* or *var. cavendishii*. You may have an indoor plant, *Hedera canadiensis var. variegata,* commonly known as "Gloire de marengo," to provide one or two long shoots. Another kind is dieffenbachia; if you have none yourself or cannot bring yourself to cut leaves off a plant, the florist will sell you one or two for your arrangement. The graceful, slightly hairy feathers which lend a light and airy appearance come from the feather grass (*Stipa pennata*), which can be grown here in water plots. The little sister of feather grass, esparto grass (*Stipa tenaciosima*), which is grown in Morocco and Algeria, is sometimes imported.
The most important thing about an arrangement of this kind is to make sure that you put some flowers at the bottom, so that the whole gives an impression of fullness and none of the holding material or sphagnum is visible. The pretty leaves of the dieffenbachia and variegated ivy form graceful descending lines.

Sunny colours in the cold

The container: Small containers on a tall or short stem are indispensable when flowers are scarce and therefore dear.

The holding material: To make sure that the thin stems of the flowers can be fixed easily in the correct positions in the quite wide neck of this glass, a few conifer twigs about as long as the cup is high should be pushed in upside down. Two pieces of strong binding wire pushed crosswise through these branches and bent round the edge of the glass ensure that the greenery does not fall away when the flowers are inserted. The transparency of glass makes artificial holding equipment a less attractive proposition. The yellow crab-apple which peeps out from under the greenery at the bottom of the container is a pleasant finishing touch, which must be applied at the outset.

The arrangement: This hazel, *Corylus avellana contorta tourtosa,* puts forth very prettily twisted branches, which have a distinctive decorative value, especially in the winter months when the tree is bare. One or two twigs are used to give this arrangement a line that fans out gracefully upwards and sideways. This pretty creation proves that you can use a bunch of chrysanthemums to make a number of small but certainly not thin skimpy arrangements. A few twigs with small flowers and buds are inserted high in the container, and the larger flowers are placed towards the bottom. A few sprays of the elegant heath *Erica gracilis* are added; their little white flowers ensure that the whole blends perfectly with the colour scheme of the room. The bottom is filled with twigs of Japanese ornamental quince *(Chaenomeles japonica),* to which some fruits of *Malus floribunda* or *Malus spectabilis* may be added. Both of these yield yellow crab-apples; the former has white-and-pink blossoms, while the latter has bright pink ones. These apples are stuck on binding wire and tied together in a bunch. Other available berries or fruits may, of course, be used in this way.

Tulips and marbles January

The container: Aquarium tanks or modern coloured glass variations on this theme are obtainable in all shapes and sizes: low and high, square and rectangular, narrow and broad, and made of thin or quite thick glass. They make excellent containers for a modern flower arrangement placed in one corner of the tank.

The holding material: For holding material, take a piece of Oasis or Mosette. You may, of course, use a metal pin-holder; before you put this in the water, wind green tape round the edge to hide the pins. To keep the block or pin-holder in position and as an additional decorative element, put a layer of specially made glass balls in the tank! Alternatively, filch a good handful of marbles from your children's bag. Marbles or plain tinted glass balls have a pleasant effect if you let daylight or lamplight shine through the container from behind.

The arrangement: All you need is a bunch of ten tulips. Choose a long-stemmed variety, since the slender stems, bent into shape with binding wire, contribute a great deal to the decorative effect. Darwin tulips are most suitable, and they are available in an infinite number of beautiful colours. If you prefer pink ones, four to ask for are Clara Butt, Preludium, Smiling Queen or Aristocrat. These are all more or less plain-pink varieties. To bend the brittle stems into shape, use green flower binding wire; this is pushed into the stem an inch or two below the flower, looped and then wound round the stem as close as possible to it. Wind the wire tightly round itself a few times at the foot of the freshly cut stem, and cut off the unwanted end with old scissors. Tulip stems prepared in this way can be fixed in graceful shapes, but please be gentle! Start with the longest stems, and carry on with flowers having shorter and shorter stems. The shortest tulips do not need to be stiffened with wire. Cut the last two flowers off quite short; one is inserted just above the water, and the other in it at an angle. A flower of contrasting colour, in this case a deep wine red sweet-william (*Dianthus barbatus*), placed right at the bottom will provide a piquant contrast.

The first shrubs are in bloom January

The container: A flat bowl with a hollow in the middle in which a pin-holder or holding material fits is quite suitable for an arrangement of a few branches. You will not usually wish to strip those first brave flowering plants in the garden. You would have to pick far too much to fill a vase, and it would not have to be too small either, in view of the sturdy form of the wood.

The holding equipment: For one of these arrangements, you could easily use a heavy pin-holder fixed in the dish with the aid of some plasticine. If you do not use too many branches, a piece of Oasis cut to the size of the hollow would also be suitable. But remember that you cannot go on making holes in this plastic material for ever; you must be sure of the right place for insertion, especially if you are using fairly thick wood. A ball of sphagnum, tied together and anchored round the edge of the bowl by means of strong binding wire pushed through crosswise, will also give good service. Make sure that the wire does not protrude, but can be covered by overhanging flowers.

The arrangement: The witch hazel, *Hamamelis mollis,* comes into flower in January to March (followed rather later by the Japanese hazel, *Hamamelis japonica,* in January to April: the former has rather larger flowers, while the latter blooms more abundantly.) Its stout branches with their tufts of yellow petals are excellent for an arrangement, requiring little else in the way of flowers. As far as the ascending and lateral lines are concerned, they have sufficient decorative value. To give the heart of the arrangement rather more weight, a few sprays of mimosa may be added; *Acacia dealbata* blooms on the Riviera in February and March. Remember to moisten the holding material with warm water in which some yellow Chrysal is dissolved. Otherwise the little balls will not be fluffy. (Unfortunately this is not possible if a metal pin-holder is used, because mimosa Chrysal and metal do not agree.) A single golden gerbera daisy will fit wonderfully well into this springtime yellow arrangement, and a tuft of blue grape hyacinths, which you have tied up beforehand with binding wire, will provide a pleasant contrast when placed near the bottom. If the pin-holder or holding material is visible, some holly or ivy leaves will come to the rescue.

30

Spring indoors

The container: A homely brown earthenware pot is just right for one of these gay arrangements. These glossy brown glazed pots are obtainable in a number of sizes, and they bend very well with the brown coffee cups and heat-resistant saucepans that we see so often nowadays. And so this arrangement may be used to decorate a laid table.

The holding material: Greenery is absolutely essential for an arrangement in a wide-mouthed pot. You may, of course, use artificial holding material or a good lump of sphagnum, but the former will be rather expensive, and the latter may be a little awkward, especially since you cannot start with the fragile stems (see "The arrangement"). So take branches of conifer greenery that are about as long as the container is high, push them in the pot upside down, and prevent them from falling away by pushing strong binding wire crosswise through the ends and securing it round the edge of the container.

The arrangement: Most of this cheerful spring arrangement consists of mimosa, *Acacia dealbata,* and so you should fill the pot with really warm water with yellow Chrysal dissolved in it. Start with the mimosa: narcissi, tulips, hyacinths and primrose are not so fond of these very warm footbaths. The woody branches of the forsythia (*Forsythia intermedia* or *F. spectabilis*) and the bog myrtle may then be worked in. The bog myrtle, *Myrica gale,* flowers in April to May with shining brown catkins, which give off a wonderful perfume if you rub them between your fingers. It is worth while to hunt for this plant, especially on damp, acid soil, where it grows wild. In any case, the florist will be sure to be able to supply a few sprigs. With their reddish brown colour, these have great decorative value even before the catkins come out. When the water has cooled off to hand warmth, you may put in the stems of narcissi and tulips; bicoloured cottage tulips are available very early in the year, and these are known as Fireflame. Finally, to give a strong dash of colour, a hyacinth and a yellow polyanthus from the garden, with its root-ball, may be included in the arrangement. Always place short-stemmed flowers like hyacinths very near the bottom, to produce a natural appearance.

A heart for St. Valentine

The heart: To make a heart for Saint Valentine's Day, choose a piece of soft board or chipboard, draw a heart shape on it and saw it out. If you are not very clever with pencil and paper and are unable to draw an exact "equilateral" heart, then draw half a heart, fold the paper double exactly down the centre line, and cut the double-folded paper along the line you have drawn. Unfold the heart, and draw round it onto the board.

The holding material: You only need plenty of sphagnum to make this heart able to hold flowers. Spread a thick layer on the heart, and secure it by tying string round. Moisten the sphagnum well.

The arrangement: Garnette roses, which open out like bowls, are very suitable for filling the surface of the heart. The deep red of the roses and the salmon colour of the azalea sprigs make a pleasant and not too sugary combination of colours. The azaleas are generally sold as Japanese azaleas, but their correct name is *Rhododendron obtusa.* All azaleas are kinds of rhododendron, of course. When the whole area is filled with salmon-pink and red, with the deep-green patches of the azalea leaves in between, the edge should be finished off with small sprigs of conifer green, so that the holding material and the board are no longer visible. Cypress, for example, *Chamaecyparis obtusa crippsi,* with its golden-yellow tips, may be used, but *Thuja occ. woodwardi* or even small pieces of the golden yew, *Taxus baccata semperaurea,* are very suitable.

Out of the cold, into the warm

The container: A small dish that is quite deep, but not too wide, is excellent for small flowers with delicate stems. To lend height, choose a small bowl with a stem.

The holding material: As the flowers have delicate stems, the holding material should not be too tough. Loosely kneaded artificial holding material may be used; a few twigs of greenery inserted upside down are also excellent, or an airy wad of fine chicken wire.

The arrangement: If you use snowdrops, *Galanthus nivalis,* in a small rounded glass, with a stem if desired, you can insert them at an angle one by one through the narrow opening. If you wish to make an arrangement on a dish, as in the picture, you should tie the snowdrops together in threes with very thin binding wire and insert these little bunches in the greenery, through the meshes of the chicken wire or into the holding material. Snowdrops have such natural charm that a formal arrangement would be a contradiction. An attractive rounded shape is best for these first outdoor flowers. If you wish to have a colour contrast, buy a bunch of blue grape hyacinths, *Muscari armeniacum.* These are inserted low enough not to disturb the line of the pretty, drooping snowdrops. Some ivy leaves will hide any visible greenery or holding material.

Narcissi   February

The container: Flowers with thick, straight stems like narcissi are best placed in a rounded container with a wide mouth, so that they can be inserted at an angle. For narcissi, irises and that sort of flower, your collection should therefore certainly include an attractive rounded pot, like this brown glazed one.

The holding material: This arrangement of narcissi has a large number of thick but rather soft and breakable stems. You should therefore not use too much greenery, and it should be firmly anchored. Cut some branches of conifer that are about as long as the pot is high, do not put too much in the pot, but make sure, if necessary with a star of strong binding wire, that the greenery cannot sink down when you start arranging. Above all, do not use too much greenery, or you may damage the wide stems. A light wad of meshed chicken wire may also prove useful.

The arrangement: Towards the end of February, the perfumes of many kinds of narcissi fill every flower shop. Ordinary yellow trumpet daffodils, and also the creamy white trumpet Mount Hood, the charming Music Hall, with a white perianth and dull-yellow trumpet, and even Mrs. R. O. Backhouse, which has a white perianth and apricot trumpet. Then there are the charming bunch-flowered narcissi, for example the Poetaz hybrid Geranium, with its white perianth and golden orange cup, or the dwarf *Narcissus triandus* Silver Chimes, which has clusters of six to eight flowers of white and soft yellow. Do not forget the fragrant jonquil, with one or two small deep-yellow flowers. If you wish to have other sweet-smelling varieties, try *Narcissus odorus plenus,* with deep-yellow, full flowers, *Narcissus odorus* Orange Queen, which is a splendid deep orange, and *Narcissus* Trevithian, with clusters of lemon-yellow flowers. These sweet scents combine wonderfully with the fresh, spicy smell (a real smell of spring!) of the trumpet daffodils. If you indulge in an exuberant display of narcissi so early in the spring you will have a whole week of pleasure, for these flowers, which are reared in hothouses, are usually offered for sale when they are still in bud. Later in the year, in April, when the narcissi bloom in the garden and the bought ones are cheap, you may treat yourself to this arrangement over again.

Hothouse flowers

March

The container: The delightful thing about flower-arranging is that there are hardly any rules to tie you down. Long stems need not always remain long, nor do short stems need to be "lengthened" by a container on a stand. If you feel like making a luxuriant flat bowlful, then you may, even with long branches and tulips.

The holding material: It is easiest to fill the bowl with a few blocks of Oasis or some other artificial holding material. As this is quite expensive, you may fill the bowl entirely with sphagnum, and then cut a piece of fine chicken wire which is three quarters of an inch larger all round than the top of the bowl. This chicken wire is secured round the edge of the bowl with strong binding wire; this arrangement ensures that it is not visible.

The arrangement: The loose plumes of soft pink-mauve and white lilac (*Syringa vulgaris* hybrids), the green and white globes of the guelder rose, *Viburnum opulus,* and purple tulips are all forced early in hothouses, to give you a chance to enjoy these spring flowers in advance. A very pretty purple single early tulip is Van der Neer; this is followed a little later on by the Triumph tulip Purple Star, and then the handsome Darwin tulips Greuze, Pilgrim, and Demeter, which is purple with a metallic blue glow. (These tulips are raised in the hothouse practically at the same time; this information is in case you wish to make this arrangement later on when they flower in your own garden.) Begin by cutting off the lilac sprays very short, but slantingly and with a sharp knife. If you wish, you may crush the short stems by tapping them gently with a hammer. Arrange the clusters loosely, so that one or two hang gracefully over the edge. The guelder roses should be about half as high as the lilac clusters, and then they will not disturb the supple line. The same applies to the tulips. Most of them are arranged so that the flowers do not project beyond the lilac, and one or two are even put very near the bottom, so that they completely conceal the holding material or chicken wire. A few gracefully drooping leaves of the curly fern *Nephrolepsis,* with their handsome bold green, emphasize the delicate combination of colours in this arrangement. A bunch of ornamental grass, tied together with binding wire, lends lightness to the ascending line. Use a few blades of *Holcus lanatus albo variegatus,* but if this is unobtainable take one or two narrow blades from your spider plant, *Chorophytum comosum,* your Portuguese grass, *Stenotaphrum,* or your carex. These are all indoor plants, but they grow so luxuriantly that two or three blades are not missed.

From garden and hothouse

The container: Even a simple basin or dish from your tea or coffee service may be used as a container. Filled with holding material, it will be admirable for a pretty arrangement of short spring flowers.

The holding material: To enable a dish to hold small flowers with delicate stems, such as blue grape hyacinths and snowdrops, you should use loosely kneaded plastic holding material. A light ball of sphagnum covered with fine chicken wire secured over the edge or a light wad of fine chicken wire may be used.

The arrangement: Both the cold soil and the warm hothouse have co-operated in the birth of this arrangement. The last snowdrops, *Galanthus nivalis,* the first blue grape hyacinths, *Muscari armeniacum* and dwarf irises, *Iris reticulata,* together with a few ivy leaves, come from the garden. Add to these a few deep-red Garnette roses and pink and white roses, together with one or two sprays of lily-of-the-valley, *Convallaria majalis,* from a warm hothouse. The latter and the snowdrops naturally project above the rounded outline, so that the graceful line of these small white flowers is shown off excellently. The flat, open red roses are placed at the bottom, together with the soft pink roses. In the heart of the arrangement the irises lend a dark note, which is repeated many shades lighter in the colour of the blue grape hyacinths, whose length is exactly between that of the roses and the snowdrops. The ivy leaves round the bottom conceal the holding material or chicken wire. An attractive feature of this arrangement is that it fits in with the colours of the surrounding objects, such as the loud red of the radio set, the plastic dishes and the salt-sprinkler.

Subtle play with twigs

The container: A flat bowl with a deeper hollow in the centre is excellent for arranging a few branches.

The holding material: A weighty lead pin-holder is very suitable for holding steady this kind of top-heavy arrangement. Dry the dish and pin-holder very carefully, put a piece of plasticine into the bottom of the dish, and place the pin-holder on top. Press it down well, so that it is firmly attached. If you have no heavy pin-holders, a firm ball of sphagnum will do the trick if it fits exactly in the hollow and is tied down with binding wire.

The arrangement: March and April see the flowering of the winter hazel, *Corylopsis spicata,* with its gracefully drooping and fragrant light-yellow flower clusters. You may expect at about the same time to see the twigs of the *Pieris floribunda*, perhaps better known as andromeda, with their firm, erect white flower clusters. Pluck one branch from each bush and let them speak for themselves in a subtle arrangement. The playful, supple line of the branch of winter hazel and the stiff, straight pieris make a pleasant contrast.

The bare base of this arrangement demands attention, of course. The pin-holder or holding material must not remain visible, and the arrangement would be unbalanced if a dash of bright colour were not added at the bottom. A few pieces of pumice stone, placed half over the holding material and the edge of the bowl, lend firmness in two senses. A bright yellow lemon repeats the yellow of the flowers in a deeper shade, while a cluster of blue grape hyacinths, cut short and tied together with binding wire, and some purple deadnettle, *Lamium purpureum*, provide an attractive colour contrast.

44

Begin the spring gaily March (beginning of spring)

The container: Anything large may be used for this kind of exuberant spring arrangement. A large pottery jug, an extra-large kettle or water jug, a small milk can, a tub (with a lining, of course) or a large brown earthenware crock are all suitable. But they must be plain, because a variety of colours on a container will naturally clash with those of the arrangement.

The holding material: Conifer greenery is recommended for this large arrangement. Do not use too much, because the container has to hold a very large number of stems. Cut a few branches so that they are as long as the container is high, put them upside down in the vase and secure them with binding wire pushed through crosswise and fixed round the edge.

The arrangement: Celebrate the spring exuberantly with anything you can pick or buy. When it is still bleak, cold or wet outside, the forsythia is in flower, the pussy-willow has fluffy paws (the *Salix acutifolia* is used here), and various kinds of ornamental prunus and twigs of almond (*Prunus amygdalus*) may be bought from a shop. Start off the arrangement with these stiff branches. They lend support in the container and decide the main lines. Then come the Dutch irises (one of the bulbous irises, *Iris hollandica*). Distribute the light blue here and there, right at the top and right at the bottom. Red and orange are supplied by sturdy tulips, for example the very strong Darwin hybrid Apeldoorn, and frivolous lilies; a lily to grow indoors (the orange one is called Harmony) that comes into flower very early is now available. Yellow is supplied by various sorts of narcissi (see page 38 for their names), and right at the bottom we have deep-blue hyacinths, bright-red anemones (Anemone de Caen) and one or two anemones of a soft blue tint to provide still more variety. See that a few tulips hang gracefully over near the base, supporting them with binding wire if necessary. You may use, among others, the handsome single early orange tulip General de Wet, or Fridoline, which resembles a lily and has pale-orange petals with a deep-orange blush.

A mixed basket

The container: Baskets are excellent for flower arrangements. Of course, you must not let the basketwork get wet; that is bad for the basket and for the article of furniture on which it is standing. Try and find a tin, bowl or glass jar that fits the basket: this means that it must be at least half an inch shallower; but baskets vary, and so it is a good idea to have a roll of thick plastic material or heavy-quality extra-wide aluminium foil. It is usually enough to line it with one layer of the thick plastic or a double layer of foil.

The holding material: You should use holding material to enable you to arrange the basket easily. The simplest is a wet block of Oasis, which may be cut to size if necessary, but a ball of damp sphagnum is also excellent. Secure it in position in the basket with wire. When you are attaching the sphagnum or holding block make sure that you do not push the binding wire through the plastic or aluminium-foil lining.

The arrangement: A mixture of cut flowers, plants and vegetables or fruit make a very attractive spring basket. The African violet (*Saintpaulia*) is a splendid plant for one of these baskets, dishes or bowls. The handsome, low, round form, the pretty colour of the flowers (deep violet, pink and now even white with violet edges) and the decorative form of the fleshy leaves helps very well to fill up the bottom of the arrangement. If the basket is high enough, then you may put the plant, pot and all, on one side along the edge and at an angle. The holding material is then placed beside it. The pot will usually absorb enough moisture for the plant from the damp material pressed against it. Lilac, blue and yellow go very well with the violet of the African violet, and you do not need very much; one spray of lilac, three hyacinths (Ostara was used here, but Delfts Blue is also very pretty), one or two narcissi, a bunch of blue grape hyacinths, an iris, two lemons and a couple of mushrooms (at the side and back). Push a strong piece of binding wire through the undersides of the lemons and mushrooms to fix them in the correct positions on the holding material. The blue grape hyacinths should be tied together with thin binding wire before being placed in the arrangement.

Easter egg

The base: The easiest and quickest way to make one of these eggs is to take a whole block of Oasis and wrap sphagnum round it in the shape of an egg. Start by winding a thick layer of sphagnum along the rounded sides of the egg, and then fill in, winding string round continuously until you have a complete egg shape. Push a double piece of strong bent wire through the egg, so that a loop projects from the top, and bend the ends at the bottom outwards round the egg, so that the loop cannot slip out and the egg can be hung up.

It is best to make the arrangement when the egg is hung up, so that you can walk all round it during the process and see whether the creation is balanced and the egg shape is retained as much as possible. Before you start arranging, put the egg in a bucket of warm water, preferably with a weight on it, until it sinks; this means that the block of holding material is completely saturated, so that the inserted stems can absorb water.

The filling: The background is a covering of grey or white Iceland moss (*Cetraria islandica*). Your florist will be able to supply you with it, usually in a damp state. If it is dry and crumbly, put it in water until it is flexible. Take for example three small pieces, tie them together with wire and insert them in the egg. When all the holding material is concealed, add flowers, vegetables, fruit and nuts. Small bunches of black grapes are put on strong wire and added. You may do the same with bright-red radishes, almost black prunes, shelled walnuts (a couple at a time) and whole Brazil nuts. Now only a few flowers are needed to complete the egg. One or two large marguerites (*Chrysanthemum maximum*) are pierced by a doubled piece of binding wire, a toothpick or a pointed matchstick through the middle and hollow stem and into the egg. One or two bulbous irises (*Iris hollandica*) may be used with hardly any support. A flower of blue hydrangea (*Hydrangea hortensis*), is plucked into pieces, which are stiffened with binding wire and inserted in the egg. A few trollius flowers and a yellow lily-flowered tulip supply yellow tints. A tuft of violet-painted raffia and, if you wish, an egg-shaped paper decoration may be used to finish off the top.

A tower for a table

The base: For this table decoration you need four large flat plates or bowls and four blocks of Oasis. The bowls may be of decreasing sizes, with a round bowl at the bottom, surmounted by a large plate, followed by a breakfast plate and then by a dessert or cake plate from your service. A block of Oasis is placed between each plate, and the top plate may have two blocks tied together with binding wire, since most of the flowers will be placed on it.

First, put the blocks in a bucket of warm water until they sink and are thoroughly saturated. Then put a block on each plate, place the next plate on top, and continue until the Easter tower or tiered bowl is finished.

The arrangement: The heart of each tier thus consists of damp holding material. The flowers and twigs are cut so that they are partly inside and partly outside the edges of the plates. In the bottom three tiers they are inserted horizontally; in the blocks at the top the line is continued vertically to give the tower a graceful crown. The tallest flower should be about twice as high as the bottom three tiers together.

Violet and yellow are the colours of Easter. A very sweet-smelling combination is lilac (*Syringa vulgaris hybrid*), deep-blue hyacinths with a violet glow (Ostara), blue Dutch irises (*Iris hollandica*), a few blue grape hyacinths (*Muscari*), small fragrant bunch-flowered narcissi (Trevithian), and here and there a touch of pink heather (the early flowering *Erica mediterreana* or, later, *Erica carnea*). See that the graceful sprays of the lilac and the elegant clusters of narcissi form the outline of the arrangement and that short hyacinths and irises provide weight and fullness and also conceal the holding blocks. Some greenery may also help here, for example some leaves of *Mahonia aquifolium*. Keep walking round your tower while you are arranging it, so that it looks beautiful from all sides: it is meant to be the showpiece of your Easter table.

Blue and blue April

The container: A flat bowl is indispensable for anyone who wishes to have opportunities for variation in flower arranging. You can make splendid arrangements in them, which fill a large area without demanding too many flowers, for you only need to fill the horizontal line. But an arrangement of this kind is suitable only for a low position, on a coffee table or as a centre-piece on a dining-room table. It may also be included in a group of ornaments, for example on a room-divider shelf that is not too high.

The holding material: It is easy, but quite expensive, to fill the bowl with some blocks of holding material cut to size or kneaded. You may also use sphagnum. This may be packed in a piece of fine-meshed chicken wire and then placed in the bowl; the piece must, of course, fit exactly. Alternatively, spread a piece of fine-meshed chicken wire over the bowl. It will be difficult to fix it to the straight sides, however, so that one of the first methods is recommended.

The arrangement: The forget-me-not is one of the first plants to flower from seed. The light blue of these little flowers is therefore often used for contrast with a group of tulips or late-blooming narcissi. Its Latin name is *Myosotis hybrida*. It is easiest to tie forget-me-nots in bunches of three or five sprigs and then insert these in the holding material. First fill the entire bowl with forget-me-nots and then place a deep-blue anemone (anemone de Caen) here and there. If you can find it in your heart to cut the flowers of an African violet, a few of these round the edge will blend in most attractively with this colour combination. You may put an entire plant, root-ball and all, at one side, or put three plants round the arrangement. In that case, start with the plants, and then fill in with the holding material.

An arrangement of blossom   April

The container: For a big arrangement of flowering branches, look out one of your largest containers, if necessary a very large *cachepot,* milk can, or small cask lined with tin to make it water-tight. If you wish to use a cask permanently as a container, make sure it is always damp, so that the wood fits quite tightly and does not leak. You may even use wooden rainwater barrels.

The holding material: Although many large branches are used in this arrangement, you should start with a fair amount of conifer greenery, especially if you are using a wide-mouthed container like the large *cachepot* shown here. The branches should be about as long as the pot is high. Insert them upside down and fix them with strong binding wire pushed through crosswise and wound round the edge of the pot.

The arrangement: Anything that bursts from the bud at this time of the year may be used in one of these blossom arrangements. Picking branches with buds on them will prolong the pleasure you gain from the arrangement indoors. Branches of ornamental fruit trees may be combined with those from useful ones. Among the ornamental ones are cherry (*Prunus avium*), peach (*Prunus persica*), apricot (*Prunus armeniaca*) or almond (*Prunus amygdalus*). Japanese ornamental cherries are, of course, celebrated. They include *Prunus kanzan* (or *Pr. serrulata*), *Prunus amanogawa* with its pillar-like growth and soft-pink blossoms, and also the straight twigs, full of pink buds, of the dwarf almond, *Prunus triloba plana.* The common crab-apple (*Malus pumila*) and various ornamental crabs (*Malus varieties*) may also be included, and naturally a few touches of green to relieve all this lovely leafless pink and white. At the bottom of the arrangement put a couple of branches of *Mahonia aquifolium,* with blossoms if you wish; the yellow makes a fresh contrast. You may also add a few twigs of other youg greenery, for example quite young leaves of the horse-chestnut (*Aesculus*). An arrangement of this kind may be tall and have a vigorous line, and it may fan out very widely, but if the branches are too close together the various blossoms will not be shown off to full advantage.

Rhododendrons and guelder roses

The container: A large glass bowl on a stem is a very useful member of the collection of containers. It has two advantages: you can make a fairly high, well-filled arrangement with not too many flowers. Only the horizontal plane has to be filled.

The holding material: Luckily, this thick green glass reveals little of the holding material, and if you have some overhanging flowers you may even use green plastic blocks. If you find it too expensive to fill a bowl of this kind with holding blocks, take a large lump of sphagnum, which is secured round the edge of the bowl with binding wire pushed through in the form of a star. Or spread a piece of fine-meshed chicken wire, which is about three quarters of an inch, over the top of the bowl.

The arrangement: Start with the large, rounded umbrellas of the rhododendron. Pink Pearl has been used, but there are many other beautiful pink or rose-red rhododendron hybrids, for example the deep-pink Cosmopolitan and the rather more softly tinted Princess Marijke. A quiet colour scheme is provided by a second rhododendron, *Azalea mollis*, known officially as *Rhododendron japonicum* or *Rhododendron molle*, of which a white variety has been used. The green and white snowballs of the guelder rose, *Viburnum opulus*, form a delightful contrast. Arrange these snowballs evenly all round, and let them overhang to give more relief. Very deep-purple tulips, which bloom late, are inserted above this green, white and pink bed to form a fascinating colour contrast: try the Darwin tulip Queen of the Night.

May flowers

The container: Even articles of everyday use, like this handsome antique butter dish, are excellent for a flower arrangement, adding to the charm of a gift. A cup and saucer, gravy boat or vegetable dish may be treated in the same way.

The holding material: Artificial holding material, cut to size or kneaded, is quite suitable for filling the butter dish, but you will be just as quick with a ball of sphagnum. This must be firm; roses have sturdy stems and are quite top-heavy. Fix it in place with strong binding wire.

The arrangement: This is a simple arrangement, and it can easily be copied by children for a present. It has twenty salmon-pink roses; this one is called Dominant. The blooms that are the furthest open (and are the darkest) are cut short and used at the bottom; the rather lighter buds are placed higher up. The yellow-and-green tinted sprigs of lady's mantle, the alchemilla, are much prettier than the usual asparagus greenery; they are therefore appearing more and more frequently in florists' shops. Alchemilla is a garden plant, which grows very easily, seeds itself abundantly and has very decorative silver-grey-green leaves with wavy edges, besides the yellow-and-green plumes of flowers. In rain and dew, thick drops like pearls lie in the centres of the leaves. In the old days, alchemilla was credited with great miraculous powers. The sprigs are put in high and low among the roses and they should also hang over the edge, giving a light and airy appearance to the whole.

Lilies-of-the-valley

The container: As we pointed out in the first chapter, your collection of containers should include food pots. A very attractive example is this French mustard pot, which is suitable for all kinds of small flowers, from the homely buttercup to the refined lily-of-the valley.

The holding material: You need none or hardly any for this kind of narrow-necked container holding quite a large number of flowers. One or two small sprigs of greenery may perhaps be put in the pot, or you may start with a couple of leaves of the lilies, which usually provide enough support. If you wish to have fewer flowers, push a piece of fine chicken wire into the container, so that the flowers may be arranged in an airy fashion.

The arrangement: A simple bunch of lilies-of-the valley (*Convallaria majalis*) has a charm all its own as a change from all the bright spring flowers. They bloom outside in May and you can pick them to your heart's content in your own or a friend's garden. But these sweet-smelling flowers are grown in hothouses throughout the year for wedding decorations, so that you can indulge in one of these delightful bunches in the middle of winter. They are expensive then, so the wad of chicken wire will come in useful. Do not forget to ask for the leaves as well. They will come in handy to fill in the arrangement and they are light green, forming a subtle colour combination with the white flower sprays.

Flowers in a basin

The container: If you fill the basin in the passage or cloakroom with an arrangement at a party, you may be assured of an unusual decoration. It also has the advantage that it cannot topple over, however many guests brush past it. This basin will show what a delightful container you can make of it. If you take the trouble to look round junk markets, bric-à-brac shops and similar places, you are sure to find an old-fashioned wash basin without much difficulty. It can be attached to the wall anywhere you wish and used as a bowl for plants or flowers. Make sure the plug fits well, and, for perfection, see that the tap fills the round opening made for it.

The holding material: The best holding material is a large lump of sphagnum, which may be secured with strong binding wire bent round the edge of the basin. Alternatively, push in a wad of fine chicken wire and secure it round the edge here and there with strong binding wire to prevent the arrangement from toppling over when the basin is full.

The arrangement: To make a combination of flowering plants and flowers, strat by putting a plant, such as the geranium used here, in the chosen position in the basin, pot and all. To make sure that it is not killed by an excessive amount of water, put the pot in a plastic bag, but leave the top open so that the soil can breathe. Then fill the basin with sphagnum or chicken wire and pour in water, making sure that it does not rise above the edge of the pot and enter the plastic bag. In this mixed arrangement, the flowers have been put in groups, so that the characters of the different colours and flowers stand out clearly. The centre is formed by deep-blue Dutch irises (*Iris hollandica*), emphasized by a single, full and rounded soft grey-blue hydrangea (*Hydrangea hortensis*). The strong colour of the upright geranium is balanced by a gracefully drooping cluster of red tulips. Round this heavy centre we have the light colours of pale-yellow snapdragon *Antirrhinum majus grandifloris* Eldorado, a cluster of buttercups (*Ranunculus acer*), and sprays of white hawthorn (*Craetaegus oxycantha*), which flowers in April to May, or, later on, the common hawthorn (*Craetaegus monogyna*), which flowers in June.

Lilac and pink

The container: All kinds of wide bowls may be used for a large, wide and not too tall arrangement. The soup tureen used here is a fine example.

The holding material: First, of course, the bowl is filled with holding material. You may use a wad of fine chicken wire. Cut a piece that is twice as large as the bowl; if the bowl has a diameter of ten inches, then take a piece twenty inches long and ten inches wide. Fold it double, so that ons half it at the bottom of the bowl and the other is an inch or two below its top edge. Then press the wire a little so that it fits the bowl. Alternatively, you may use blocks of Oasis, for example one whole large block and another round it in pieces cut to size by yourself. Or have sphagnum or greenery, or a combination of a holding block with sphagnum or greenery, the latter materials being secured round the edge of the bowl with a cross or star of binding wire, so that they cannot fall away.

The arrangement: If you are using a bowl with a pattern, its colour will decide those of the arrangement. In this case, lilac and pink were chosen because of the reddish-purple pattern on the bowl. Branches of blossom and cut flowers, picked in the garden and bought at the florist's, are combined in perfect harmony. Tulips in pale clear pink and pink hyacinths represent the bulbs; and bright purple-pink anemones the corms. Some pink roses and carnations were bought. A pink hydrangea flowering indoors provided one bloom, which was placed low to give roundness to the arrangement. Lilacs prevent the colouring of the arrangement from being too sugary, and sprays of blossom make the line free and light. You may use the almond *Prunus triloba plena,* various ornamental cherries, for example the Japanese *Prunus kanzan* or *Prunus amanogawa,* or else a prunus such as the almond *Prunus amygdalus,* the peach *Prunus persica,* the apricot *Prunus armeniaca* and the wild cherry *Prunus avium.* Sprays of wild crab-apple blossom (*Malus pumila*), which have a pretty pink blush on the outside, and of various ornamental crab-apples are also very suitable. Stronger tints are provided by sprays of the Ghent azalea (*Rhododendron gandavense*) or *Rhododendron ponticum,* the wild mauve rhododendron, and the heathers that flower in the winter and spring, such as *Erica carnea, Erica mediterranea* or *Erica arborea.*

A grid full of early plants

The container: Arrangements on a grating, which may be hung up if you wish, are very attractive, because the holding block or ball of sphagnum can be attached very easily. If you can get a fine antique wrought iron grid it is an ornament in itself. But even a new grid, such as your oven rack, a metal trivet on legs, or even the salad-basket, are excellent.

The holding material: First, place on the grid a piece of thick aluminium foil folded double. Put your damp holding block on this, or else a ball of damp sphagnum, secure it to the grid with iron wire, and then press the aluminium foil up along the edges, cutting off the surplus. Of course you do not fill the entire grid, but attach the holding material in the middle or in a corner.

The arrangement: All kinds of early spring plants mixed together, flowers of course, but also vegetables and fruit, will make an attractive show. We have used two green peppers, close together and laid on the grid; push a piece of binding wire through the base of the fruit, fold it double, wind it round a few times, and push it into the holding block. Beside these, one or two asparagus stalks are attached to the holding block with binding wire, with a handsome white bulb of garlic in the middle. A bunch of garlic is placed at the back, and its dried shoots peep out from under the asparagus at the front. An onion is tied to the bottom of the grid, which is hanging up in this case, and three tomatoes in a row counterbalance the peppers on the right side. Put the first tomato on a strong piece of wire, bend round the end, so that the fruit cannot slip off, and then put on the other tomatoes. An red apple is placed towards the base of the arrangement, above the garlic, and then comes the turn of the flowers. Orange lilies and orange tulips are used. The new American lilies bloom early in the spring when grown in hothouses; they also make good indoor plants. The lily used is the bright orange Harmony; there is also a lemon-yellow Prosperity and a deep red Cinnabar. The orange tulips look very pretty here. We used the single early tulip General de Wet; the single early tulip Princess Irene is also very beautiful, with its pattern of purple flames on the outside of the orange petals. Place one cluster of lilies and one or two tulips towards the bottom of the arrangement, put the second lily gracefully at the top, and complete your arrangement with one or two tulips on binding wire, with stems of different lengths. A few slender narcissus leaves lend an airy green appearance.

One arrangement, three containers June

The container: Why stick to one container? A large arrangement in three small containers looks very attractive. Choose straight shapes. Three modern, narrow, tall glasses of the same height may be used, or three glasses of increasing heights, or three narrow earthenware beakers.

The holding material: If you are using opaque glass or earthenware, start by putting conifer twigs upside down in the containers. If you are using transparent glass, loosely tie up three bunches of greenery, cutting them to a height of some two or three inches. Hold them upside down and push two pieces of strong binding wire crosswise through each bundle a little below the top. Put a bundle of green in each glass, and wind the projecting pieces of wire of the cross round the rim of the glass, so that the bundle cannot sag. The wire will hang behind the upside down sprigs of greenery. The three containers are now set in a triangle in the place where they are to stand, and the flowers may be started. It is difficult, if not impossible, to move an arrangement whose flowers are shared between three different containers.

The arrangement: Here we have pink tulips, a few roses of different shades and sprays of bougainvillaea. In the spring, when cut flowers are still expensive, a medium-sized bougainvillaea plant is not really much more expensive than two or three bunches of flowers, and they last a long time. The well-pruned plant will send forth shoots on all sides in favourable conditions, such as a conservatory or cool greenhouse. Start by filling the two containers at the back. Place in them the longest sprays of bougainvillaea, long-stemmed tulips and some decorative greenery, for example a shoot from your umbrella plant. The tulips should be stiffened with binding wire; insert it in the stem an inch or two below the flower, make a loop, and wind it downwards closely round the stem. The following are beautiful pink Darwin tulips: Aristocrat, Smiling Queen, Clara Butt, Preludium and Peerless Pink. Work towards the front with shorter sprays, quite short tulips and a few roses; ask for Bridal Pink, a charming rose, which changes from light to dark pink at the edges. At the bottom, in the container at the front, put two roses in different shades of pink and a tulip. Hide the visible green twigs with one or two ivy leaves. Make sure that the arrangement forms a whole and not three loose bunches.

A bowl of flowers

The container: The advantage of a bowl on a stand is that a fairly tall arrangement can be made with quite short flowers. Even a very shallow white earthenware fruit bowl may be used.

The holding material: For holding the flowers in this shallow bowl, make a ball of damp sphagnum, which fits into the hollow at the bottom and is rounded at the top. Push two pieces of thick wire crosswise through the ball, and wind a short length round the edge of the bowl. Or you may use a block of Oasis or Mossette and fill in the sides with semicircular cut pieces of the same material. The holding material should also be fixed with wire. During arrangement, see that the pieces of wire are concealed by flowers put in at the bottom.

The arrangement: The graceful line is formed by the fine plumes of the astilbe, usually known incorrectly as spiraea. The dark reddish-pink astilbe Granat is used. First stick the astilbe into the ball of sphagnum or the blocks so that the plumes fan out evenly on all sides; this is an arrangement for the middle of a table, and so it must look just as beautiful from every side. You will get the best results by turning the bowl round continually while you are working on it. The pink roses, known in the shops as Carole (the dark-red variety is known as Garnette) open out like flat bowls, so that they look their best at the bottom. If you place one or two buds higher up as well, they will disturb the airy line when they open out. To provide darker tints, use a few hearts of purple rudbeckias, *Rudbeckia purpurea*, which have finished flowering; they still have a decorative value that is entirely their own. If you happen to have a cat's tail plant, *Acalypha hispida*, in your room, take about three tails. The hanging woolly pink plumes give a charming finishing touch. But the annual love-lies-bleeding, *Amaranthus caudatus*, which you may sow in your garden, can spare one or two of its reddish-purple plumes.

Warm as the summer June (beginning of summer)

The container: You need a large one for a tall, luxuriant arrangement to welcome the summer. A big brown earthenware pot, a green-painted metal pail or a painted metal milk can are excellent. The milk can like the water jug has the advantage that the neck is narrow, making a wide-spreading arrangement easy.

The holding material: First, place upside down in the water a few branches of conifer greenery, which are about as long as the container is deep. Do not use too much, because summer flowers have quite thick stems and will therefore quickly fill the space.

The arrangement: You have an infinite number of large and warmly coloured flowers to choose from. You may have a riot of colour or a careful choice as in the picture, in which lilac, rose-red, mauve and blue have been used. For a big arrangement of this kind, the round heads of the alliums (*Allium aflatunense* or *Allium albo plumosum*) and the sturdy spikes of the foxglove are excellent. Handsome new varieties of the latter include *Digitalis gloxinoides,* with large flowers resembling gloxinias, and *Digitalis horizontalis,* which has flowers round the stems. Use some seeded foxglove stems to lend a note of green: these, together with the seeded spikes of delphiniums, are often much easier to use for green tints than leaves, especially at the top. The third leading member is the delphinium, in various shades of blue. The airy mauve plumes, which prevent the arrangement from becoming too heavy, are sprays of *Veronica incana* or *Veronica spicata* (the latter also being known as "erica"). Among the large centaureas, which belong to the cornflower family, various kinds are used for edging and in borders. Very beautiful and well-shaped examples are the lilac, pink or bluish balls of the knapweed *Centaurea jacea, Centaurea calcitrapa,* and *Centaurea rhenana.* The sturdy green that supports this stalwart arrangement is provided by the horse-radish, *Cochlearia armorica.* Other suitable leaves for this purpose are those of the hogweed (*Heracleum*), and the silver thistle, *Onopordon.*

A gift in a glass

The container: If you give one or a set of glasses for a birthday or wedding-present, it will be appreciated still more if you make a flower arrangement in the single glass or in one of the set. They make charming table decorations. Put one by each plate, and your party table will look more festive than ever.

The holding material: For a table decoration, place a small pin-holder on edge at one side, after winding green adhesive tape round it so that the pins are mostly concealed. For a gift glass, secure a piece of holding material (Oasis or Florapak) or a ball of sphagnum at one side, if necessary with the aid of binding wire wound a short distance round the edge of the glass.

The arrangement: You do not need large quantities of flowers. One or two sprays of blossom, twigs from bushes with small flowers: broom, potentilla, *Magnolia amabilis, Kolkwitzia amabilis,* garden hibiscus, *Deutzia gracilis, Chaenomeles* (japonica), buddleia or sprays of fuchsia, supplemented by some green and a contrasting colour, are all you need. This graceful arrangement has three sprays of fuchsia, a pink rose and rosebud set deep in the glass, one or two African violets (*Saintpaulia*) above them, some blades of white-edged ornamental grass (*Holcus lanatus albo variegatus*) in between and graceful fans of conifer greenery; juniper, thuja and lonicera are suitable. The glass is only half-filled with water, because sphagnum or Oasis absorbs enough water for the flowers, which may be quite short. The rose is therefore mostly above water. A few glass balls and one or two large marbles provide an unexpected note.

Variation on the arrangement of wild flowers

The container: Seize any opportunity of laying hands on an old white water jug. Their design is perfect for arrangements, and all flowers look beautiful in white. As they are usually wide with a narrow neck, it is quite easy to make a handsome, spreading arrangement.

The holding material: Because of the narrow necks you will need little greenery, if any. If you are not yet very experienced, use one or two branches of conifer greenery, which are about as long as the container is deep, and insert them upside down. The first flowers, even if they are smooth-stemmed and top-heavy marguerites, will then stay in position immediately, and you can give your arrangement the right shape at the outset.

The arrangement: This bunch of wild flowers borrows its great charm from the fresh combination of colours: white (marguerites), red (poppies) and blue (cornflowers), with the graceful forms of various kinds of corn in between (oats, wheat and barley). If you are unable to pick your wild flowers in the country, you can create a very attractive variation with flowers from the garden and some grasses or one or two oat stalks that have gone astray along the road. If you find any poppies, pick them, and do not forget some buds and even dead flower-heads; they are fine, if only because of the frequently capricious shapes of the stems. The bergamot, *Monarda didyma* Mahogany, for example, will also provide some bright red. White marguerites are to be seen in nearly every garden, and they are cheap everywhere. Blue is supplied mainly by delphiniums, the perennial variety or the annual larkspur *Delphinium ajacis,* one or two monkshoods or *Aconitum,* ordinary cornflowers, *Centaurea cyanus,* or else the larger mountain cornflowers, *Centaurea montana,* and perhaps one or two irises and hardy geraniums (*Geranium grandiflorum* Johnson's blue). Even when these geranium flowers have fallen, their stems will give line to the arrangement. This is repeated in tufts of milfoil (achillea Perry's White), and the line is filled in and made lighter by one or two oat stalks and some soft green ears of grass, for example Yorkshire fog, *Holcus lanatus,* the common bent, *Agrostis tenuis,* or quaking grass, *Briza media,* all of which are wide and airy.

Summer colours in a teapot July

The container: Your collection is bound to include a big old teapot. Its fine rounded form is excellent for a well-rounded arrangement which is not too high. Plain whites are quite difficult to find and therefore usually quite expensive. Pots with a small flower decoration are not such a problem, but their colours must not clash with the arrangement.

The holding material: First, put one or two branches of conifer greenery in the container upside down. Cut them long enough to prevent them from falling into the teapot, but short enough to prevent them from projecting very far at the top, if at all. To make sure that the flowers do not push the greenery down, insert two pieces of strong binding wire crosswise through the branches, and wind the ends a short distance double round the edge of the pot. As their openings are usually not so wide and the stems of the summer flowers used are quite thick, you will need very few of these conifer twigs.

The arrangement: Start with the long plumes of the narrow-leaved bell-flower, *Campanula persicifolia.* These are thick and not too heavy, and so they will easily stand up in the greenery. They are followed bij giant snapdragons (two shades of pink are used: *Antirrhinum majus grandiflorus rosella* and *Antirrhinum majus grandiflorus celestial)* and the almost white pink roses picked from the rambler The New Dawn, which blooms all summer. These roses are put at the base, so as not to disturb the graceful line of the campanula and snapdragon spikes. Although the large alliums, *Allium aflatunse,* grow on very long stems, they have a very rich effect if the stems are cut very short, and the thick lilac balls are used to give the arrangement "body". Put them in after the roses. If they go in earlier, it will be very difficult to get these heavy flowers, which are apt to fall over, in the correct places and positions. Finally, smaller balls on quite long stems are inserted. Centaureas, as here, are excellent. They include the rosy purple knapweed, *Centaurea jacea,* the star thistle, *Centaurea calcitrapa,* and *Centaurea rhenana.* These also supply leaves, which underline this arrangement with their pretty indentations and silvery undersides.

Quiet yellow to loud orange July

The container: Both new enamelled kettles and old iron ones make fascinating containers. The advantage of a black kettle is that you are not tied to any particular colour. What is true in the case of white holds good for black as well: any flowers, any shapes and any colours look beautiful. The robust black shape underlines the bright colours of this orange and yellow arrangement and makes them still more dramatic.

The holding material: You will not need a great deal of this; the bushy giant Africans provide plenty of support. Insert one or two branches of conifer greenery upside down in the kettle. See that they are not too short, but do not let them project more than half an inch above the edge of the kettle. Push two pieces of strong binding wire through crosswise, and wind it a short distance double round the top edge of the kettle. This will prevent the greenery from falling away when the flowers are put in.

The arrangement: The basis is formed by stout branches of the giant African marigold, *Tagetes erecta flore plena*, which comes in four colours, deep orange, light orange, butter yellow and soft yellow. You may grow them yourself from seed. The light-orange variety has been used here. Their branched form provides good support for the arrangement. The homely yellow clusters of helenium, *Helenium pumilum aurantiacum*, make it friendly; the proud foxtail lily, *Eremurus bungei*, provides the beautiful line. If you continually remove the dead flowers from these torches, you will enjoy the eremurus for a long time, because all the flowers open out, right to the top. A couple of soft-yellow carnations and a single rose of the same tint lend lightness at the bottom. Touches of green are supplied by the yellow-speckled leaves of *Aucuba japonica variegata* and the seed heads of delphiniums.

Blue with and without prickles

The container: Flat bowls are excellent for a low arrangement, to be looked at from above. A pleasant, harmonious whole is created by selecting shades of a single colour for the bowl and flowers.

The holding material: It is easiest to use a block of Oasis, Florapak or Mosette, which may be cut to size as desired. Or you may even use one very large or three smaller pin-holders made of metal.

The arrangement: A very beautiful result can be achieved by different flowers in shades of the same colour. The basis of this arrangement is formed by African violets (*Saintpaulia*) of two different colours, one bluish-violet and the other purple. The plants are put in the bowl with their root-balls, the rest of the space being filled with pieces of Oasis. If you do not use plants, but only cut flowers, the bowl may be filled as described above. The darkest tints are those of the irises (*Iris hollandica*), which are placed low down; the lightest are the scabiouses (*Scabiosa caucasica*), of which one or two are put in right at the bottom, while a few flowers and buds spread out gracefully above the arrangement. The rounded heads of the globe thistle, *Echinops ritro*, strike a comical note, and the graceful sprays of the sea holly, *Eryngium hybridum*, provide the supple line. If you are friendly with a botanical gardener or other grower of special plants, you may be lucky enough to procure a blue flower of *Eryngium alpinum*, and give your arrangement a special character. If not, the flowers of the teasel (*Dipsacus*) or one of the thistle species (*Onopordon arabicum* or *acanthium*) will also blend in well with this colour scheme.

From the grass verges

The container: You must use your imagination if you are going to make a good collection of containers. A small perfume bottle is charming for a few snowdrops, a light-blue cream pot for yellow pilewort, an old bottle of a special shape for a single rose, a mustard pot for the little flowers picked for you by your children, an a rusty, dented iron bucket (a "bricklayer's bucket") for a gaily-coloured arrangement from the grass verges.

The holding material: You may start by putting some greenery in the bucket upside down, but not too much, for you can pick as many wild flowers as you like, and the stalks are usually thick and juicy, and will soon break if the container is crammed too full.

The arrangement: Wherever grass grows on the verges, flowers grow as well. Colourful poppies, radiant white marguerites, yellow buttercups and tansies (*Tanacetum vulgare*), the blue of cornflowers and alkanet (*Anchusa officinalis*), and also the pink and lilac of the rose-bay willow-herb (*Epilobium angustifolium*), flowering rushes (*Butomus umbellatus*), ragged robins (*Lychnis floscuculi*), and hemp-agrimony (*Eupatorium cannabinum*) may all be used. Do not despise the seed tufts of the agrimony, the charming downy and silvery-pink balls, which may be found everywhere in August and September on swampy ground, and look very effective in an arrangement of wild flowers or even with more expensive flowers. Whatever colours you may be able to obtain, the main theme will usually be provided by umbelliferous plants, flowering in whites, pinks or yellows, or green and stiff after the seeds have formed. They look beautiful in any arrangement, even with cultivated flowers from the garden or the florist's. In the picture on page 101, they are used with orange dahlias. Umbelliferous plants may be found throughout the year. It starts with the delicate cow parsley, *Anthriscus silvestris,* the healing caraway, *Carum carvi,* and the fragrant creamy sweet cicely, *Myrrhis odorata.* These are followed by the speckled hemlock, *Conium maculatum,* which is very poisonous and may be recognized by brown spots on the stems, the wild carrot, *Daucus carota,* and the coarse-leaved ever-present ground elder, *Aegopodium podagraria.* Finally, from July until the autumn you may find the flowers of the sturdy, pinkish wild angelica, *Angelica silvestris,* the much more graceful marsh hog's fennel, *Peucadanum palustre,* the largest of all, the giant hogweed, *Heracleum sibiricum,* the burnet saxifrage, *Pimpinella saxifraga,* and along the water side the large water parsnip, *Sium latifolium.*

All in white

The container: Plenty of small dishes and bowls may be found in every household. Small china bowls, flat drums, glass dessert dishes, small jugs or heat-resisting bowls are all suitable flower containers and will display your most special flowers to full advantage.

The holding material: It is quite easy to prepare one of these flat bowls. Put in one quite large or three smaller metal pin-holders, fill the bowl with a piece of Oasis, cut to size; or make a ball of sphagnum, wind string round it, push strong flower-binding wire through it crosswise, and wind the ends round the rim of the bowl.

The arrangement: If you wish to show very special flowers to full advantage, see that the colours of the arrangement harmonize with the shade of the main flower. In our picture, two sprays of species delphiniums are the eyecatchers. You will not find them at every grower's, but they are certainly worth the trouble to find. The large, flat, orchid-like flowers, white or cream, need a quiet background, and so only white shades have been chosen for this arrangement. You may use, among others, the cluster roses of the climbing (or weeping) "White Dorothy Perkins", with their vague pink blush, dead-white flower tufts of the milfoil (achillea Perry's White), the silver leaves and flowers of the lamb's ears (*Stachys lanata*), the Siberian edelweiss, *Anaphalis triplinervis* or the everlasting flower, *Anaphalis margaritacea,* and *Siderita candidans.* If you are unable to obtain white delphiniums, make an arrangement on one of these low white bases with a few tuberoses (*Polianthes tuberosa*) or a couple of Cape hyacinths (*Galtonia candidans*). The tuberose has erect, bell-shaped and wonderfully sweet-scented flowers; Cape hyacinths have large hanging bells on stems that may be as much as a yard high.

Cheap and dear go well together

The container: There are now so many attractive enamelled kettles of all colours on the market that you should add at least one to your collection, and preferably several of different colours and sizes, as kettles, which are roomy with narrow openings, make excellent containers. It is a very good thing to have one available for every kind of flower. What is more, a kettle is not finished for good when you put flowers in it for a week. Just clean and scrub it thoroughly, and you can use it again for water for your tea or coffee.

The holding material: First, cut a few branches of conifer greenery according to the height of the kettle, put them in water upside down, and push two pieces of strong binding wire through their ends. Wind the wire round the rim of the kettle, to prevent the greenery from flopping.

The arrangement: Three flowers of the red Cape lily, *Haemanthus katherinae*, were used for this very beautiful arrangement. They are not cheap, but they keep for a long time in water. If you have a conservatory or cold greenhouse, then you can bring this bulb into flower yourself. Sprays of the common sorrel are placed among the expensive *Haemanthus* flowers. This field sorrel, *Rumex acetosa*, and you will see it growing everywhere along the roadsides in the country, produces spikes that turn from green to rosy and rust-brown tints. Both their colour and shape makes them excellent for use in arrangements, for example with grey-blue scabiouses or pink chrysanthemums. They have a rather more special effect than asparagus, rhododendron leaves or oak branches. A few of the long narrow notched leaves of the false aralia, *Dizygotheca elegantissima*, are put in low down, and an African violet has been placed in the heart. You may cut the flowers and leaves of this plant, but if you knock it out of the pot and carefully place the small root-ball in the centre of the arrangement, you will be able to pot the plant again with a bit of luck later on and continue to enjoy it.

Two flowers in one colour August

The container: No collection is complete without a dark-green glass cup. The deep green provides an attractive foil for any arrangement in light tints, which might otherwise be a little too charming.

The holding material: It is best not to use any light-coloured plastic blocks in dark glass; they will be seen and have an unnatural effect. Cut a few conifer branches off short, so that they do not project more than half an inch above the edge of the cup when they are inserted upside down. Take two strong pieces of binding wire, push them crosswise through the branches, and wind the ends a short distance round the edge of the cup.

The arrangement: The special feature of this one is that two quite different kinds of flower harmonize with each other, because they are practically the same colour. Never be too conventional when choosing your flower combinations. At first sight, it might be said that the coarse gladioli and refined hybrid tea roses do not go together, but in this composition these two extremes complement each other excellently. There is a wide choice of salmon-coloured gladioli, for examples Copper King, which is salmon-copper with a vague white tinge towards the heart, Orange Giant, in a rather deeper salmon orange, Bon Voyage, which is azalea-pink with a salmon-coloured glow, Long Island, a soft salmon with a small red spot in the throat, Happy End, in salmon-pink with a cream spot, Hochsommer, with its orange-salmon flowers with a brownish-orange glow, and Picardie, which is salmon-pink with an apricot glow. The choice of roses is rather smaller. You will be able to buy in the shops at about this time a soft-salmon hybrid tea rose (perhaps Chic) and a rather darker orange-salmon tinted one (this is Sonora). In the garden, you may be able to cut the large, cream-coloured rose Casanova, Peace, which blushes from salmon to pink, or the floribunda rose Elizabeth of Glamis, which has dark-salmon flowers. Choose two kinds which harmonize best. Do not use the gladioli too high on their stems; place the open roses towards the bottom of the arrangement, and the buds and half-opened roses halfway up. This ascending arrangement can be given a graceful descending curve in the form of a cluster of berries of the snowy mespilus (*Amelanchier canadensis*), *Amelanchier spicata* or the bird-cherry (*Prunus padus*).

Sunflowers

The container: You naturally need a large one for these tall beauties. You may use a fine dark-brown earthenware pot, a tall copper kettle or a painted milk can. The Dutch "apple kettle" shown in the picture has its "holder" to fit into the ring of a coal stove. The kettle would have been too low for this tall sunflower arrangement, but the holder remedies this. See if you can find something rather like this. Do not hesitate to use it even if it leaks; a small plastic bucket or large tin inside will soon put this right.

The holding material: As sunflowers are top-heavy, the kettle or leak-proof lining should first be filled with quite a lot of conifer branches as long as the kettle is deep. If you provide greenery only at the top the flowers will topple over, because they will find no support at the bottom. As sunflower stems are very stiff, firm insertion in the greenery raises no problems. Fix the greenery at the top by pushing two strong pieces of binding wire through crosswise and bending them a little way round the edge of the kettle.

The arrangement: What is more summery than a luxuriant arrangement of sunflowers? The light-yellow rays with their dark or light brown centres are sturdy and gay, warm and fresh at the same time. If you have no container or room suitable for such a large arrangement of *Helianthus annuus*, you can make a smaller but just as festive display from *Helianthus* varieties that form branched plants with smaller blooms, such as *Helianthus annuus intermedius*, for example Bronze King, with its brown and brownish-yellow flowers. Or you may use *Helianthus nanus fl. pl.* Golden Globe, which has double flowers, or *Helianthus cucumerifolius stella*, with its small light-yellow flowers with black centres. An attractive dash of colour may be provided at the bottom by sprays of berries, such as those of the guelder rose *(Viburnum opulus)* used here. Or you may have branches of elder-berries, the red mountain elder, *Sambucus racemosa*, or the purple-black common elder *(Sambucus nigra)*.

Dahlias in a flat-iron

The container: Filling old or new articles of every day use with flowers opens up a new world of possibilities. You will immediately view your stock from a fresh angle and discover that your collection of containers is much larger than you thought. Take one of these old flat-irons; it may have been used as an ornament for years, and you have been looking at it every day. Fill it with flowers and you will get extra enjoyment from the combined beauty of flowers and ornament.

The holding material: Articles that are sensitive to water or have holes in them must first be lined with thick plastic, which must not project at the top or be otherwise visible. Then fill the inside with a ball of damp sphagnum or a block of Oasis or Florapak cut to size. The holding material may be fixed along the edge with binding wire, but that will not be necessary with an arrangement of light, short flowers like the one in our picture.

The arrangement: The Top-Mix dahlias, which were invented for small gardens, have a charm all their own. They have the true, simple dahlia form, but are no larger than two inches across; they bloom abundantly on plants a foot high. There are beautiful pink varieties. A couple of roses are used at the bottom to conceal the holding material; three roses are also put rather higher up. Never be afraid to cut a few flowers very short, especially with an arrangement like the one illustrated. Otherwise you will have flowers all round, but however beautiful the form may be, you will always be looking at a colourless green heart, in which conifer twigs, a holding block or sphagnum are too often visible. Get used to the idea of not only picking perfectly sound, well-opened blooms, but also some buds and even an occasional overblown flower. These will give the arrangement a genuine and living air often lacking in an arrangement of pure, irreproachable beauty.

Late roses

The container: A flat glass bowl with a rather deeper hollow in the middle is excellent for a low arrangement. Have a few pretty stones or large pebbles in your container cupboard: they can be very useful for concealing the holding block or pin-holder, and provide variation in your arrangements.

The holding material: The hollow in the bowl may, of course, be filled with a ball of damp sphagnum or a block of Oasis cut to size. Alternatively, you may use a large metal pin-holder, or in this case, in which a few stems of floribunda roses are inserted, you may even try a perforated globe.

The arrangement: Roses are always beautiful: in the spring, when the first blooms of the first flush unfold, and in the summer, when the second may be even more luxuriant. But in September, when the late roses bravely defy wind and weather, they have a moving charm of their own. The last roses are so dear to us. They are a little stained by rain and wind; they look a little pinched and not very large; and yet it is in the autumn, when the gaudy colours of the dahlias predominate, that a small arrangement of soft-tinted roses is something quite special. Go into your garden, and pick any roses you see: they may well be shattered in the next downpour or storm. You may put a few in a narrow glass or bottle, but you can also make a low arrangement of them. A few flowers will make quite a large one. Make sure that any pin-holder, holding block or sphagnum is concealed by flowers or a couple of clusters of heather (erica). It is best to tie up the thin sprigs of heather with thin binding wire. This is particularly advisable if you are using a metal pin-holder or a perforated globe. One or two large and smaller stones may help to hide the base of your arrangement and give it quite a different look.

The autumn is coming September (beginning of autumn)

The container: You need large containers for large dahlias, and containers that can stand steadily, because the flowers are heavy. Suitable examples are large earthenware jars, large pottery jugs or pots, and heavy, preferably cast-iron kettles. If you use a white water jug, an ordinary tall vase or an enamel jug, you must make it heavier by pouring in a good layer of sand or fine gravel.

The holding material: The container, with its sand or gravel if any, is now filled quite full with upside-down greenery. Not so full that the dahlia stems, which are much more delicate than those of sunflowers, can hardly be pushed in, but full enough for the very top-heavy flower stems to be held in the right positions. Two pieces of strong binding wire, pushed crosswise through the underside of the branches and bent round the edge of the pot, ensure that the greenery does not fall about during arrangement.

The arrangement: Herald the autumn with a tawny bunch of orange dahlias. The colours of autumn are golden, yellow, orange and apricot, and the dahlia is the autumn flower *par excellence.* Among orange semi-cactus dahlias like these, you have various very beautiful varieties to choose from. There is the apricot Hazard, Anneke Grönloh with its pepper-orange glow, Renaissance, which is orange with a red glow, Cadans, which produces deep-yellow flowers, and Golden Heart, with really bright orange blooms. Always start one of these large arrangements of flowers with vulnerable petals at the bottom. If you try to add the lower flowers later, you will find it hard to work them in. It is much easier to slide in the longer stems neatly between the others. A very fine result is achieved by a combination of the orange of the dahlias with the greyish green of large seed umbrellas. This is more out of the ordinary than a conventional combination with oak leaves, which are troublesome to gather and supplied in much too small quantities in the shops. A drive or walk along a country road or the waterside will yield an unlimited quantity of seed umbrellas from large umbelliferous plants such as the cow parsnip, *Heracleum sibiricum,* the wild angelica, *Angelica silvestris,* the marsh hog's fennel, *Peucadanum palustre,* or the large water parsnip, *Sium latifolium.*

100

Contrast composition

The container: Old soup tureens are certainly worth keeping or procuring. They are ideal for a full arrangement that fans out widely. If you have different ones, with different-coloured patterns, always choose colours that match in with those of the flowers.

The holding material: Holding blocks may be used for filling; one of these will be needed whole, and another in pieces cut to size to fill in the openings round the first block. You may also use a ball of sphagnum or a combination of sphagnum and greenery, secured to the edge of the bowl by a cross or star of strong binding wire. But a wad of fine chicken wire is also ideal. Cut a piece that is twice as large as the bowl, fold it double, put one side into the bowl, bend the other side round, gently, so that it remains an inch or two below the top edge of the bowl, and press it in a little, so that it fits the shape of the bowl and cannot tip up.

The arrangement: Pompom dahlias with their determinedly rounded heads are splendid in a mixed arrangement, but they also look very fine on their own in a large, wide display, but not in a dull, straight container in which the flowers stand stiffly side by side. Here, pompom dahlias in two contrasting colours have been used: the dark Moor Place or Darkest of All and the light-pink Allegonda or Lampe. But other contrast compositions will look charming, white with red, yellow with purple, orange with white or lilac with purple. To soften the stiff, taut line of the arrangement, twigs of ripe and unripe blackberries have been added.

Autumn harvest October

The container: When flowers become scarce and stems become short in the late autumn, a cup on a tall stem should be used for a tall arrangement; this will give you half your height before you even start. Green glass provides a fine neutral basis for most colours, and for soft tints it is often better than white earthenware, or colourless glass, which has a rather too sugary effect.

The holding material: In transparent containers it is best not to use light holding blocks, which will be visible through the glass. You may put a large, heavy metal pin-holder at the bottom, perhaps winding green adhesive tape round the edge to conceal the pins. But it is preferable to use conifer greenery, cut to the size of the cup, inserted upside down and fixed with a wire cross.

The arrangement: It is a real adventure to go into the garden in October. Not much seems left, but if you look carefully you may discover the delightful faded green and pink flowers of the hydrangea, *Hydrangea paniculata grandiflora*, which fill the arrangement splendidly and give it a quiet charm. And the buddleias, now no longer visited by butterflies, will still have one or two spikes of flowers. The violet *Buddleia davidii*, Empire Blue and the purple-red variety Royal Red flower for a long time. Your liatris will have made a brave attempt to come into flower a second time, and the cosmos you have sown yourself (*Cosmos bipinnatus dazzler*) will also have a few late flowers. Take everything, and be thankful that no night frosts have spoiled your pleasure. There are also plenty of roses for sale at the florists, such as the lilac-tinted Sterling Silver; buy a bunch, and you have everything you need for this charming arrangement. Start with the hydrangeas: they fill in well and form the line of the arrangement. Then put in the roses, and finally distribute the rest of the buddleias, liatris and cosmos so that you have a gleam of purple everywhere.

Berries in a bottle October

The container: Bottles and carafes of different sizes, colours and materials are excellent for an arrangement of a few flowers. Red and white wine, salad dressing, vinegar and so on are often sold in very attractive bottles nowadays and some kinds of *vin rosé* are marketed in handsome earthenware bottles.

The holding material: You do not need any, of course, for a container with such a narrow neck. Generally speaking, you only have to push the stems through it. If you happen to have some space left, so that the heavy branch of hips leans over, fill in with a small, short piece of greenery.

The arrangement: A week may be devoted to the charming branches of the Japanese *Rosa rugosa,* with its huge orange-red hips. This generous bush provides material for arrangements on two occasions, first the flowers and then the highly decorative fruit. Several species roses yield delightful hips of all shapes, usually from light orange to deep red. Other shrubs, such as the service tree, *Sorbus torminalis,* and the guelder rose, *Viburnum opulus sterile,* come in handy; a few clusters of these have been used here. Other berries may be included, such as the rowan, *Sorbus aucuparia,* the various berberis species, the elder with black berries, *Sambucus nigra,* and the mountain elder with red fruit umbrellas, *Sambucus racemosa,* the glittering firethorn, *Pyracantha coccinea,* and the sea buckthorn, *Hippophae rhamnoides.* Or, choose the fruit of various *Malus* species, the brilliant crab-apples, or hawthorn berries; try the beautiful oriental hawthorn, *Crataegus orientalis,* with red-blushing, deep-yellow, large fruit. Or you may prefer the cotoneasters. But do not forget the extremely beautiful fruits of the spindle tree, *Euonymus europaeus,* with its shining orange seeds peeping out of deep-red capsules. In this arrangement, we have used useful as well as ornamental fruit, a spray with fruit of the American blueberry (an improvement on the usual bilberry, *Vaccinium corymbosum*), a few cooking pears on wire at the bottom. The only flowers are one or two sprays of orange freesia; and seed umbrellas of the spirea (the true one, the bush).

Subtle autumn

The container: Any large pot or jug whose colour blends in with the mature colours of this arrangement may be used, provided that the opening is wide, so that all the branches and flowers can fan out widely.

The holding material: You may use a wad of fine chicken wire for this wide-necked pot. Cut a piece twice as high as the pot and a little wider, fold it loosely double and press it together a little. Push it into the pot so that the wire is about an inch below the edge and therefore invisible. You may, of course, use greenery inserted upside down in the familiar way. Do not have too much: there will be a great many flower stems and twigs.

The arrangement: The pink and greenish umbrellas of the hydrangea, *Hydrangea paniculata grandiflora*, are strikingly beautiful in the autumn, and they fill up the arrangement splendidly. So do the rounded umbrellas of the more usual hydrangea, *Hydrangea hortensis;* one bloom with a soft greenish tinge is placed at the bottom. The whole arrangement is made up of subtle pink tints and green shades. From the garden come sprigs with red berries from *Pernettya mucronata*, sprigs of pink snowberry, *Symphoricarpus chenaultii*, and some from the American blueberry. Various heathers are also in flower now in the garden, for example *Erica carnea* Winter Beauty and *Erica tetralix*. If you cannot get any of these, use some sprigs of the indoor heather. *Erica gracilis*. If you have a passion flower, *Passiflora coerulea*, outside, do not be afraid to take one or two shoots; the plant is evergreen. You may also find one or two Michaelmas daisies in the garden, such as the delightful light-lilac *Aster amellus* Oktoberkind or the large clusters of the lilac and blue *Aster novi-belgii* Royal Blue. Only now do you need to go to the shop to buy flowers. Choose shades of pink that blend with the flowers selected from your garden, such as the marguerite-flowered autumn chrysanthemum, *Chrysanthemum morifolium hybridum*, and six or seven roses. This is a very beautiful new rose called Dixibelle, whose outermost petals have a greenish glow.

Arrangement of berries October

The container: When flowers are dear and berries in the garden are scarce, choose containers that will make the largest and highest possible arrangement from a little, in other words a container on a stand. This amber glass specimen is an attractive neutral example.

The holding material: With glass, it is best to use greenery, which shows a natural green colour, or a piece of fine-meshed chicken wire spread over the opening of the cup.

The arrangement: When choosing shrubs for the garden, be sure to include some that bear berries. For a beautiful, wide and not too high hedge, for example, why not select the snowberry (*Symphoricarpus*), which is always quite cheap. There are several varieties. The best is *S. albus leavigatus,* which yields thick clusters of white berries, and then there is *S.* White Hedge, which has a rather more compact growth. In our arrangement we have used *S. chenaultii,* which has charming pink-blushing berries; *S.* Magic Berry has darker lilac-red fruit. And of course there are the various barberries (berberis). These berries are very sour, which is why birds are generally kind enough to leave them on the bush. A pleasant feature of the berrying berberis species is that the leaf turns very pretty colours in autumn; there are also evergreen barberries but they do not usually set fruit. Wear gloves when picking barberry twigs: the thorns are very sharp. The pernettya, *Pernettya mucronata,* bears its thick white or pink berries at this time of the year. If you cannot find it in your heart to pluck twigs from the garden, most florists can offer shrub branches. A blue note is provided once again by sprays of the American blueberry. At the bottom there is a thick cluster of *Malus* fruit; look out for the crab-apple *Malus pumila* John Downie, with its large yellow and red fruit. These are first tied together with binding wire before being put in. To lend weight to the heart of this arrangement, which would otherwise be too thinn, add some salmon-pink roses, together with a single gerbera daisy of a rather darker salmon tint. The various sprays of berries spring from this heart of flowers.

All in orange

The container: A large green glass jug is used for this orange arrangement. It is just right for a sturdy, warm-tinted display.

The holding material: Greenery can be seen fairly clearly through the green glass but chicken wire or artificial holding material would be still more conspicuous, and so greenery, inserted upside down and fixed round the edge with a cross of binding wire, is the right material. A cover of fine-meshed chicken wire spread over the opening of the jug will also be very useful and at the same time remain invisible.

The arrangement: Once again, the garden and florist have co-operated. The firethorn, *Pyracantha coccinea,* has let us have one or two beautiful branches, and so has an ornamental malus (*Malus floribunda* and *Malus spectabilis* both yield yellow fruit). One or two ivy leaves and twigs of the gold-splashed and evergreen *Elaeagnus pungens* var. *maculata* or *aureo-variegata* support the arrangement. Before the night frosts begin you may find a few pompon dahlias in light or dark orange. Your florist will supply you with the beautiful orange marguerite-flowered autumn chrysanthemum *Chrysanthemum morifolium hybridum,* and orange lilies. Lilies are now brought into flower in hothouses almost the whole year through.

The last leaves from outside

The container: You need a very low bowl for a leaf arrangement, which is always looked at from above.

The holding material: A large pin-holder is placed against one side of the bowl. A piece of pumice stone is laid beside it for a more natural effect.

The arrangement: Even if it is too cold for flowers in the garden, there are still a few beautiful leaves, some ornamental grass and fruit-bearing conifer twigs. Nearly all varieties of the juniper *(Juniperus* species) have bluish frosted berries, usually on the undersides of the twigs, and so these are placed wrong way up. The thin blades of the ornamental Yorkshire fog grass, *Holcus lanatus albo-variegatus,* give an airy ascending line, which is needed above the heavy leaves at the bottom. Beautiful leaves are provided by the lily-of-the-valley, *Convallaria majalis,* the marsh-marigold, *Caltha palustris,* the sweet flag, *Acorus calamus,* the arum (usually called "calla", but the official name is *Zantedeschia;* the variety *albi-maculata* has white spotted leaves) and, of course, the variegated *Hosta fortunei.* You may also use leaves from sunflowers, *Helianthus annuum,* cannas or begonias. Look along grass verges and ditches for the hogweed *(Heracleum)* and the large water plantain *(Alisma plantago aquatica).* Take some long narrow leaves of the yellow flag, *Iris pseudocaris,* as well. The large leaves, with or without variegated edges or spots, are almost horizontal, so that they are looked at from above; this makes them as decorative as possible. Lily leaves and the ornamental grasses stand erect above them, together with one or two sprigs of juniper.

Simple piece

The container: A very low dish, which merely serves to hold a pin-holder and water, is an ideal neutral base.

The holding material: A heavy pin-holder anchored to the dish with a piece of plasticine or modelling clay is perfect. You hardly need any pebbles or marbles to conceal the pins: the base of the arrangement sees to that.

The arrangement: The nerine, a relative of the amaryllis, also known as the Guernsey lily, which comes from the Cape and Japan and blooms at this time of the year, may be rather expensive; but it is very strong, lasting for over two weeks, and you need only three of these graceful pink lily clusters to make this decorative pin-holder arrangement. The official name of this bulbous plant is *Nerine sarniensis*, and there is another kind with larger, deeper-pink flowers. Cut the stems, of the nerines to very different lengths, the tallest being about twice as high as the shortest, and the third one in between. Stiffen the ends of the stalks with thin binding wire, otherwise the pins of the holder may break up the fleshy stems. so that the flowers topple over. First arrange the three nerines, and then the ornamental grass (*Holcus lanatus albo-variegatus* from the garden or the stiff narrow cream-striped leaves of *Carex,* from indoors). Make bundles of the grass with fine binding wire; put some upright beside the nerines and some almost horizontal and pointing forwards. A solid base for this delicate arrangement is provided by the heart of an ornamental cabbage; you can buy seed of variegated ornamental cabbages and sow them yourself; the variety Yuka has splended white leaves with very crinkled edges. One or two pieces of the stalk of this cabbage are used at the back to conceal the pin-holder. A single rose (if possible Dixibelle) is placed at the bottom, and three ornamental red-striped leaves of *Maranta tricolor* complete the fan at the base from which the nerines rise.

Old tints in new flowers

The container: Dark-green glass is a beautiful, quiet basis for this autumn arrangement. The foot ensures that the whole does not become too heavy.

The holding material: Use a few branches of conifer greenery of the right length, so that they just fit in the container; insert them upside down, and fix them with a cross of binding wire. If the glass is very thick and therefore not very transparent, you may use a wad of chicken wire or spread a net of fine-meshed wire over the opening of the container.

The arrangement: All "autumn chrysanthemums" that we buy are hybrids of *Chrysanthemum morifolium.* Every year new varieties and new colours appear, so that a chrysanthemum arrangement can be created in every shade of a single colour. The deep-purple cluster chrysanthemums, the large soft-pink ones with rust-coloured hearts, and the very fine-petalled ones of a delicate lilac hue form a subtle combination. Among all those flowers with radiating petals, seven pink roses form a very pleasant contrast, and a few nerines lend an exotic air. Round the outside, there are some airy shoots with seed tufts of the traveller's joy (*Clematis vitalba*), which grows in the hedges and has small white flowers from June to August. Do not forget to place some of the flowers near the bottom, to give more dimension and conceal all those green stems. Note the bowl with sweet-smelling dried rose petals – another way of getting enjoyment from flowers.

From the tropics

The container: This time a small wooden tray acts as your "container". An arrangement can be created in one corner.

The holding material: To avoid damaging the tray by prolonged damp it is advisable to place a thick piece of plastic under a ball of sphagnum. It is easiest to make one of these arrangements with a ball of sphagnum; wind wire firmly round it and secure it with binding wire round the edge of the tray. If you wish, you may use a small tin or dish with a heavy pin-holder fitting in it exactly. The sphagnum or dish should be completely covered by the fruit and seed capsules at the base of the arrangement.

The arrangement: Orchids are imported nowadays from various tropical countries, to continue their growth in hothouses. Some are quite cheap, especially when we consider their long life in water. The ones in the picture are sure to live for three weeks; they are sold as arachnis (*Arachnis moschifera*, also known as the spider orchid). There are various shades of orange, red and brownish, all of which produce attractive flowers resembling butterflies. The twigs usually have a natural, graceful curve, making arrangement very easy. To lend some weight to the base, fruits of two kinds of quince have been used, the green, pear-shaped common quince, *Cydonia oblonga*, and the yellow, apple-shaped ornamental quince, *Chaenomeles japonica*. A single bunch of the African violet (*Saintpaulia*) provides a strong dash of colour; ivy leaves lend a touch of deep green, and the tulip seed capsules complete the base.

Mingled coppers

The container: Copper or bronze-coloured kettles are ideal for an autumn arrangement in very warm tints. It is quite easy to arrange flowers in one of these pot-bellied kettles, and it will give them a beautiful full, rounded line.

The holding material: Insert a little greenery upside down in the kettle, and fix it round the edge with a cross of binding wire. The flowers used have thick stems, and the opening is fairly narrow, so do not use too much.

The arrangement: When it is bleak and cold outside and the fire burns cosily indoors, you really need a warm-coloured arrangement to make you remember that thousands of flowers will spring from the earth which is now as hard as iron. Autumn chrysanthemums allow us to make an arrangement in various shades of the same colour throughout the winter. All those copper colours mingled together, from the lightest brass to red copper and even bronze, produce a delightful winter combination; and there are so many different flower forms: small, tightly-filled cluster chrysanthemums, marguerite-flowered cluster chrysanthemums, the "fried eggs", with their large hearts and short crowns of petals and, of course, the big mop-heads to give strength to the arrangement. A few sprays of the Chinese lantern plant, *Physalis franchettii*, have a pleasant effect at the top and bottom, and branches of the common quince, *Cydonia oblonga* and japonica, the ornamental quince *Chaenomeles japonica*, underline the arrangement. If you have none of these warm tints, make up this arrangement in white. Choose a white earthenware or porcelain holder and any white chrysanthemums; you will find plenty. To underline your creation, you may then use some white *Pernettya mucronata*, if you wish with one or two white or green ornamental gourds (*Cucurbitaceae*) threaded on wire.

New ideas

The container: You will need a cup with a stem for this drooping arrangement.

The holding material: This will have to support a great deal, for example bunches of grapes, and so it should be anchored very firmly. Fill the cup tightly with artificial holding material cut to size or kneaded, or with a good firm ball of sphagnum. Stiffen the whole by pushing a star of thick binding wire through the holding material, and bend the ends round the edge of the cup. A cover of chicken wire, to keep everything firm, is also ideal; the candles just pass through the meshes.

The arrangement: Do not be too conventional when selecting material for your flower arrangement; think up new ideas, and do not hesitate to include fruit. Bunches of small white grapes are not very expensive at this time of the year. They are put on strong binding wire, which is pushed deep into the holding material, so that the bunches cannot sag. If you wish, you may start with the grapes, push the wire right through, and bend it back a little on the other side. Before the arrangement is too full, place one or two Christmas or Lenten roses (*Helleborus caucasicus purpureus*) quite high up, close to the four purple candles, which are set in the heart. The pink is repeated in one or two real roses and in sprays of pink pernettya, *Pernettya mucronata*. Keep the flowers short, to make a compact, rounded arrangement. If it is for the middle of the table, keep walking round it while you are arranging to make sure that it looks right on every side. Fill in with a few twigs of fir, which may project airily. If you can get at the charming Colorado spruce, *Picea pungens*, use some of that. Some young, glossy brown leaves of mahonia, *Mahonia aquifolium*, hang down on the underside. Finally, add some gracefully drooping eucalyptus twigs, so that they spread out all round. One or two shorter eucalyptus twigs, placed higher up, ensure that the blue and grey are distributed evenly.

124

Start the winter like this December (beginning of winter)

The container: A simple glass container in the form of a diabolo will enable you to manage with a fairly small number of branches without any extras. Many sundae glasses are this shape.

The holding material: It is difficult to use holding material with a container of colourless glass, because it will always be visible. This one has a pink layer in the glass which saves the situation.

The arrangement: It may have looked like it for a long time, but now it is winter officially. But do not let this make you unhappy: December is a wonderful month, it is full of festivities, and snow looks beautiful in the garden, even if it is a nuisance on the roads. To celebrate the white of winter, have a radiant arrangement, perfumed by the very first white lilacs raised in hothouses. Three sprays are enough. For variation, you do not want subtle shades, but a fresh, piquant contrast of white with red, orange and green. Green is provided by holly *(Ilex aquifolium)*. There are twigs with berries and leaves on them, one with no leaves, only berries, and some variegated holly. Gracefully curving coral sprays from the scarlet plume *(Euphorbia fulgens)* from Mexico lend lightness, and one or two red carnations provide balance below.

126

Christmas begins at the front door

The base: Any florist can sell you a hoop or ring and this is an easy base for a Christmas wreath. Twigs of fir are tied round the wreath with green string or green binding wire. It is easiest to use one long wire, so that the twigs neatly follow the circle of the hoop. Firmly wound balls of sphagnum are now secured at three points, for three clusters.

The filling: Sprigs of berry-bearing holly, *Ilex aquifolium,* and variegated holly are inserted at the three points. *Ilex aquifolium aureo-marginata* has gold-variegated leaves, while *Ilex aquifolium argenteo-marginata* has white-patterned ones. The holly is accompanied by mossy twigs, eucalyptus and various kinds of fir cones; bleach one or two for a pleasant colour scheme. Pieces of Iceland moss, *Cetraria islandica,* which your florist will supply, are placed in the centre of each cluster for emphasis. If it is dry and crumbly when you get it, put it in water first until it is pliable and easy to handle again. Both the fir cones and the Iceland moss are put on strong wire. Wind a loop round the bottom edges of the scales of the fir cones; tie three pieces of Iceland moss together. They are then inserted firmly in the sphagnum. Tie a bow of red ribbon, and that is all you need to do for this decorative wreath, which will last for weeks and show everyone that Christmas begins at the front door in your house.

Christmas ball   December

The base: For this Christmas ball, you should first make an egg-shape from an oval wad of chicken wire. Round this wind a thick layer of damp sphagnum, with green string or binding wire tied round it. Do not forget to make a strong loop of wire at the top of the chicken wire, so that the ball can be hung up immediately. This loop will naturally project through the sphagnum. A ball of this kind may be used for dried flowers, when the sphagnum may be allowed to dry out, or for flowers needing water. In the latter case, the layer of sphagnum should be very thick and the flowers very short-stemmed, so that they do not reach down into the waterless chicken wire. The Christmas decorations need no moisture or hardly any, so that you do not need to worry about them.

The filling: The ball is covered with pieces of Iceland moss, *Cetraria islandica*, on wire, fir cones, walnuts, small clusters of green grapes and blue frosted berries of the *Chamaerops*, a kind of palm which yields these currant-like fruits in the tropics. The green is provided by leaves of variegated holly (*Ilex aquifolium aureo-marginata*) and very short and rather longer twigs of three kinds of spruce fir, the blue (*Picea pungens*), the common (*Picea abies*) with short needles, and the Serbian *(Picea amorica)* whose needles are set rather more loosely. Holly with berries is placed at the top, and a sprig of eucalyptus stands out here and there, preventing the effect from being too stark and stiff. The large orange fruits of a tropical solanum are imported nowadays from southern regions at Christmas time; they are the size of a mandarin, have a prickly corolla and stem and keep for a very long time. They make a fine dash of colour threaded on binding wire; push double wire through to the underside of the fruit, pull it through and loop the two ends round each other. Four of these fruits, threaded on binding wire one above the other, are hung from the ball. You may, of course, use mandarins instead.

A Christmas decoration on a shelf December

The base: This Christmas decoration can be placed wherever you wish to add a note of gaiety. You can make it in a jiffy. Saw a piece of soft board, chipboard or wood to the right size, line it on the underside with plastic or thick aluminium foil, and fix a firm ball of sphagnum on the top, or else a piece of artificial holding material cut to size. You can make in the same way decorations for tables, stairs or the edge of a mirror. For a mirror you will not need a board; just attach a ball of sphagnum or holding material and, on the underside, plastic or foil.

The filling: Two kinds of palm from the tropics come to our aid during our Christmas: the *Chamaerops* with soft-grey to blue berries and the date palm *(Phoenix dactylifera).* Their overhanging fruit clusters give the arrangement a graceful, flexible line, so that the stiff twigs of the blue spruce fir, *Picea pungens,* and the holly, *Ilex aquifolium,* may fill the ascending and horizontal lines. The holding material is concealed by pieces of Iceland moss, *Cetraria islandica,* and small fir cones.

Gold for the Christmas table December

The container: For this golden table decoration use a container that is not too conspicuous, for example a dark green glass pot, which costs little and lets the arrangement speak for itself.

The holding material: For a change, do not use conifer greenery inserted upside down, but start by inserting branches of the blue spruce fir, *Picea pungens*, quite deep all round and so that they cross over each other. They provide sufficient support for the rest of the arrangement with quite a large number of flowers and branches.

The arrangement: As a variation on the traditional Christmas theme, have a table arrangement in gold and yellow. After the blue twigs of common fir, gold-sprayed twigs of common fir, *Picea abies*, and holly, *Ilex aquifolium*, are put in position. There is now enough support for the longer, also gold-sprayed branches with male alder catkins and female alder tufts; both the grey alder, *Alnus glutinosa*, and the white one, *Alnus incana*, yield both sorts. These airy branches form the outermost lines of the arrangement. The centre is occupied by a couple of gilded fir cones. Clusters of unripe dates, *Phoenix dactylifera*, hang down and form a transition from gold to yellow (of course you may have to use a substitute). Glossy yellow peppers (*Capsicum annuum*), one or two yellow cluster chrysanthemums and yellow roses (Dr. Verhage) are placed both in the centre and spreading out all round.

A special everlasting arrangement December

The base: It is worth using several blocks of Oasis for this tower, which will last for months or even years. The dry blocks are placed one on top of the other, cut into the shape of a cone, and secured firmly with binding wire. The cone is placed in a shaped small dish and is ready to receive the arrangement. You may also make a cone out of fine chicken wire pressed together. A layer of sphagnum is wound round this, not to provide the dry cones and seed capsules with moisture, but because it is not so easy to make an arrangement on a chicken-wire cone. The sphagnum is secured with green string or binding wire.

The filling: The various kinds of opium poppy (*Papaver somniferum*) have very decorative rounded seed capsules with star-shaped crowns. They are excellent for an everlasting arrangement like the tower in the picture. Of course, seed capsules from other flower-bearing plants are also very suitable when they have been throughly dried. There are the large capsules of tulips, and also the elegantly pointed ones of ragged robins, and others. Fir cones are another very important part of the filling. There are very many attractive small cones, such as those of the larch, *Larix decidua,* the Japanese larch, *Larix leptolepsis,* and the Douglas fir, *Pseudotsuga douglasii.* But decorative cones may have to be bought, such as the very fine-scaled cones of the Japanese cedar, *Cryptomeria japonica,* and the rounded ones of the swamp cypress, *Taxodium distichum.* The greyish-blue cones are found on the different kinds of incense cedar, *Librocedrus decurrens,* which grow in California, New Zealand and the Moluccas. But junipers also have some to offer; *Juniperus chinensis,* which hails from China and Japan, produces quite large light-blue fruits. Any gaps between the larger cones are filled in with these and with simple black and brown alder tufts from the common alder, *Alnus glutinosa,* or the grey alder, *A. incana.* The bottom of the tower is finished off with a few tips of conifer greenery, for example golden sprigs of *Chamaecyparis obtusa crippsii,* and one or two clusters of very small dried flowers; these are from Mexico.

Dry in summer, enjoy in winter

The container: You should be very careful when you are choosing the container for an arrangement of dried flowers. You will be looking at it for a long time, and so the container must be very handsome, like this beautifully shaped piece of pottery.

The holding material: You need very little for one of these narrow-necked containers, preferably none at all, or the delicate stems of the last flowers are sure to break. If you are not very experienced, put a layer of plastic holding material or sand at the bottom of the container, so that the first flowers stay in the correct positions immediately. Your holding material and sand should, of course, both be dry.

The arrangement: Even with dried flowers, you can make an arrangement in different shades of one colour. Various tints of pink have been chosen here. The small double pink flowers of *Acroclineum roseum* are beautiful for this. Like the larger *Helichrysum bracteatum monstrosum plenum,* you can easily sow and dry this plant yourself. Pick the flowers when they are at their height, hang them upside down, and leave them to dry in an airy, dry room. The varieties Purpureum (dark purple), Rosy Gem (light pink) and Silver Rose (light pink) have been used; the flowers of all these are in various stages of openness. On the underside the arrangement is finished off with branches of the perennial statice, *Limonium tataricum.* The "shoots" are formed by dried spikes of the annual pink larkspur *Delphinium ajacis* and the dried seed pods of love in a mist, *Nigella damascena.* The last are very decorative, because the carpels, which coalesce with each other, turn greenish pink. Here and there a space is filled by a bunch of grass, for example the thick, woolly, pink Yorkshire fog *(Holcus lanatus).* Deep down in the heart there is a dash of violet in the form of a few sprigs of annual statice *(Statice sinuata* var. Midnight Blue).

138

Flowers from the world

The container: An arrangement of dried flowers has the great advantage that it can be placed in a container with a leak. You may use an old copper or bronze vessel, for example, and it doesn't matter if it leaks.

The holding material: First seal any leaks on the inside if you are using sand. A layer of dry sand or dry Oasis is then most suitable.

The arrangement: Nearly every part of the world has played its part here, for dried flowers and seed capsules are flown to us from high mountain ranges and the tropics. The garden has provided autumn flower heads of the hydrangea, *Hydrangea paniculata grandiflora*, honesty seed-pods, *Lunaria annua*, creamy-white helichrysum, *Helichrysum bracteatum monstrosum plenum* var. *schneeball*, a single seed torch of the monkshood, *Aconitum napellus*, dried twigs of the holm oak, *Quercus ilex*, with its holly-like indented leaves and a single twig of the Chinese lantern plant, *Physalis franchettii*. Their woody nature and "dry" flowers naturally make various thistles suitable. The sea thistle, *Eryngium campestre*, grows wild here, as do the woolly thistle, *Cirsium eriophorum*, or the Carlines thistle, *Carlina vulgaris*, with its marguerite-like flowers with large centres. This last thistle has a relative in the mountains: the silver thistle, *Carlina acaulis*, which opens its very large flowers in sunshine only (see the bottom right-hand corner of the arrangement) and must therefore be picked and dried at just the right moment. The mountains also supply the handsome long seed torches of the teasel *Dipsacus silvestre*, and the smaller relative of the artichoke, the cardoon (*Cynara cardunculus*). In Tibet the woolly edelweiss grows; this is a kind of leontopodium whose woolliness increases with height. But the very fluffy, rounded seed heads of our own Pasque flower, *Anemone pulsatilla*, may also be dried for this arrangement. The splendid flowers of the protea are now being flown over from Africa more and more frequently. These protea species are excellent for drying; note the large round flower in the centre. There are 130 of them, *Protea mellifera* being the best known, while *Protea grandiflora* with pink flowers eight inches across is the largest. At the mouth of the Ganges, in Ceylon, south-east Asia and tropical Australia grows *Nypa fruticans*, a palm with dark-brown round, prickly fruit measuring four inches across, a welcome acquisition for an exotic arrangement of dried flowers.

Corsage for a dress or bracelet

Method: Every flower, leaf or twig must be specially treated beforehand when you are making a corsage. The flowers are given a support in the form of fine binding wire. This is pushed into the stem just below the flower, or else it is pushed into the stem just below the flower, looped and then wound downwards closely round the flower stem, or else it is pushed through the centre, for example with roses, and then wound downwards closely along the stem. The leafy twigs are also given a support of binding wire, and even the loose leaves are treated in the same way: the wire is put through the central rib about half-way along, looped and then twisted together on the underside, so that half the leaf rests on this loop and can be bent into shape to some extent. (This stiffening is badly needed by flowers and leaves, because a corsage has to put up with a great deal during a celebration day or evening.) All the flowers and leaves are then given their own supply of drinking water at the freshly-cut bases by winding damp cotton wool round them, small pieces, of course, to avoid thick wads. Green flower tape is then wound round the flower stems, binding wire and cotton wool to make them stiffer and hold moisture better. When all the ingredients for the corsage have been prepared in this way, you may start with the arrangement. First take the main flower (here in one case a red rose, for the other a cluster of berries), and then place the other short-stemmed flowers round it. Hold the corsage against the dress or a piece of material all the time while you are working, to see whether the shape is suitable for pinning on. Carry on until all the flowers, leaves and leafy twigs have been arranged in a graceful ensemble, and then wind all the stems together again with green flower tape. If you are making a corsage on a bracelet or a hair grip, keep holding it on the wrist or in the hair to make sure that the corsage has a beautiful and wearable line. Attach the corsage to the bracelet or hair grip with binding wire, round which you have wound green flower tape to make it softer.

Index

Index of English and botanical names

Acacia dealbata (mimosa) 21, 30, 32

Acalypha hispida (cat's tail) 72

Achillea Perry's White (milfoil) 78, 88

Aconitum (monkshood) 78

Aconitum napellus 140

Acorus calamus (sweet flag) 114

Acrolineum roseum (everlasting flower) 138

Aegopodium podagraria (ground elder) 86

Aesculus (horse chestnut) 56

African marigold (*Tagetes erecta flore plena*) 18, 82

African violet (*Saintpaulia*) 48, 54, 76, 84, 90, 120

Agrostis Tenuis (ornamental grass) 78

Alchemilla (Lady's mantle) 60

Alder, common (*Alnus glutinosa*) 136

Alder, grey (*Alnus incana*) 134, 136

Alisma plantago aquatica (water plantain) 114

Alkanet (*Anchusa officinalis*) 86

Allegonda (pompom dahlia) 102

Allium aflatunse 74, 80

Allium albo plumosum 74

Almond (*Prunus amygdalus* and *Triloba plena*) 46, 56, 66

Alnus glutinosa (common alder) 136

Alnus incana (grey alder) 134, 136

Amaranthus *caudatus* (love-lies-bleeding) 72

Amelanchier canadensis mespilus (snowy) 92

Amelanchier spicata 92

Anaphalis margaritacea (everlasting flower) 88

Anaphalis triplinervis (woolly edelweiss) 88, 140

Anchusa officinalis (alkanet) 86

Andromeda (*Pieris floribunda*) 44

Anemone de Caen 46, 54, 66

Anemone pulsatilla (pasque flower) 140

Angelica (*Angelica silvestris*) 86, 100

Anneke Grönloh (semi-cactus dahlia) 100

Anthriscus silvestris (cow parsley) 86

Antirrhinum majus grandiflorus celestial 80

Antirrhinum majus grandiflorus rosella 80

Apeldoorn (Tulip) 46

Apple (see also Crab) 11, 68

Apricot 56, 66

Arachnis Moschifera (spider orchid) 120

Aralia, false (*Dizygotheca elegantissima*) 90

Aristocrat (tulip) 28, 70

Artichoke, cardoon (*Cynara cardunculus*) 140

Arum (Zantedeschia) 114

Asparagus 68, 90

Aster amellus (michaelmas daisy) 108

Aster Novi-belgii (michaelmas daisy) 108

Astilbe 72

Aucuba japonica variegata 82

Azalea, Ghent (*Rhododendron gandavense*) 66

Azalea, Japanese (*Rhododendron obtusa*) 34

Azalea Mollis (*Rhododendron japonicum* or *molle*) 58

Barberries (*berberis*) 110

Barley 78
Begonias 114
Bell flower (*Campanula persicifolia*) 80
Berberis (barberries) 110
Bergamot (*Monarda didyma Mahogany*) 78
Berries 9, 92, 94, 108, 110, 126, 142
Bilberry (*Vaccinium corymbosum*) 106
Bird-cherry (*Prunus padus*) 92
Blackberries 102, 106
Blueberry, American 106, 108, 110
Bog myrtle (*Myrica gale*) 32
  Bon voyage (*gladiolus*) 92
Bougainvillea 70
Brazil nuts 50
  Bridal pink (rose) 70
Briza media (Ornamental grass) 78
  Bronze king (*Helianthus*) 94
Broom 76
Buddleia 76, 114
Buddleia davidii (buddleia) 104
Butomus umbellatus (rushes) 86
Buttercups (*Ranunculus acer*) 12, 62, 64, 86

Cabbage, ornamental (yuka) 116
  Cadans (*semi-cactus dahlia*) 100
Calla (*Zantedeschia*) 114
Caltha palustris (marsh marigold) 114
Campanula persicifolia (bell flower) 80
Canna 114
Cape hyacinth (*Galtonia candidans*) 88
Cape lily, red (*Haemanthus Katherinae*) 90
Capsicum (peppers) 68, 134
Capsicum Annuum (Yellow peppers) 134
Caraway (*Carum Carvi*) 86
Cardoon artichoke *(Cynara Cardunculus)* 140
Carex 40, 116
Carlina vulgaris (carline thistle) 140
Carnations 66, 82, 126
  Carole (rose) 72
Carrot, wild (*Daucus carota*) 86
Carum carvi (caraway) 86
  Casanova (rose) 92
Cat's tail (*Acalypha hispida*) 72
Centaurea (knapweed) 74, 80
Centaurea calcitrapa 74

Centaurea jacea 74, 80
Centaurea rhenana 74, 80
Cetraria islandica (Iceland moss) 18, 50, 128, 130, 132
Chaenomeles japonica (quince) 26, 76, 120, 122
Chamaecyparis obtusa crippsii (cypress) 34, 136
Chamaerops (Palm) 130, 132
Cherry 11
Chestnut, horse 11, 56
  Chic (rose) 92
Chinese lantern plant (*Physalis franchettii*) 122, 140
Chorophytum comosum (spider plant) 40
Chrysanthemum 9, 20, 26, 90, 108, 112, 122, 134
Chrysanthemum maximum (marguerite) 50, 78
Chrysanthemum morifolium hybridum 108, 112, 118, 122, 134
Cicely, sweet (*Myrrhis odorata*) 86
  Cinnabar (lily) 68
Cirsium eriopnorum (woolly thistle) 140
  Clara Butt (tulip) 28, 70
Clematis vitalba (traveller's joy) 118
Cochlearia armorica (horseradish) 74
Colorado spruce (*Picea pungens*) 124
Cones 18, 126, 128, 132, 134, 136
Conifer branches 92, 94
Conifer greenery 16, 18, 26, 32, etc.
Conium maculatum (speckled hemlock) 86
Convallaria majalis (lily-of-the-valley) 9, 42, 62, 114
  Copper king (*gladiolus*) 92
Corn 78
Cornflower (*Centaurea*) 74, 78, 86
Corylopsis spicata (winter hazel) 44, 76
Corylus avellana contorta tourtosa (hazel) 26
  Cosmopolitan (rhododendron) 58
Cosmos (*Cosmos bipinnatus* Dazzler) 104
Cotoneaster 106
Cow parsley (*Anthriscus silvestris*) 86
Cow parsnip (*Heracleum sibiricum*) 100
Crab apple (*Malus varieties*) 26, 54, 56, 66, 106, 110, 112
Craetaegus monogyna (hawthorn) 64
Craetaegus orientalis 106
Craetaegus oxycantha 64
Cryptomeria japonica (Japanese cedar) 136
Curcubitaceae (gourds) 122
Cydonia oblonga (quince) 120

Cynara cardunculus (cardoon) 140
Cypress (*Chamaecyparis obtusa crippsi*) 34, 136

Dahlia 86, 98, 100, 102, 112
    Darkest of all (pompom dahlia) 102
Date (*Phoenix dactylifera*) 132, 134
Daucus carota (Wild carrot) 86
Deadnettle (*Lamium purpureum*) 44
    Delft blue (hyacinth) 48
Delphinium 18, 74, 78, 82, 88
Delphinium ajacis (larkspur) 78, 138
    Demeter (tulip) 40
Deutzia gracilis 76
Dianthus barbatus (sweet-william) 28
Dieffenbachia 24
Digitalis gloxinoides (foxglove) 74
Digitalis horizontalis 74
Dipsacus silvestre (teasel) 84, 140
    Dixibelle (rose) 116
Dizygotheca elegantissima (false aralia) 90
    Dominant (rose) 60
Douglas fir (*Pseudotsuga Douglasii*) 136
    Dr. Verhage (rose) 134
Dutch iris (*Iris hollandica*) 46, 52, 64

Echinops ritro (globe thistle) 84
Edelweiss, Siberian (*Anaphalis triplinervis*) 88
Edelweiss, woolly 140
Elder, common (*Sabucus nigra*) 94, 106
Elderberries 94, 106
    Elizabeth of Glamis (rose) 92
Epilobium angustifolium (willow herb) 86
Eremurus bungei (foxtail lily) 82
Erica arborea (heather) 66
Erica carnea 52, 66, 108
Erica gracilis 26, 108
Erica Mediterreana 52, 66
Erica tetralix 108
Eryngium alpinum (sea holly) 84
Eryngium campestre (sea thistle) 140
Eucalyptus 124, 128, 130
Euonymus Europaeus (spindle tree) 106
Eupatorium cannabinum (hemp-agrimony) 86

Euphorbia fulgens (scarlet plume) 126
Euphorbia pulcherrima (poinsettia) 21
Everlasting flower (*Anaphalis margaritacea*) 88
Everlasting flower (*Helichrysum Bracteatum monstrosum flore pleno*) 24, 138, 140
Everlasting flower (*Siderita candidans*) 88

Fern (*Nephrolepsis*) 40
Fir twigs 18, 124, 128
    Fireflame (tulip) 32
Firethorn (*Pyracantha coccinea*) 106, 112
Floribunda rose 98
Forget-me-not (*Myosotis hybrida*) 9, 54
Forsythia 46
Forsythia intermedia 32
Forsythia spectabilis 32
Foxglove (*Digitalis gloxinoides*) 74
Foxglove (*Digitalis horizontalis*) 74
Foxtail lily (*Eremurus bungei*) 82
Freesia 106
    Fridoline (tulip) 46
Fuchsia 76

Galanthus nivalis (snowdrop) 36, 42
Galtonia candidans (cape hyacinth) 88
Garlic 68
    Garnette (rose) 34, 42, 72
    General de Wet (tulip) 46, 68
Geranium 64, 78
Geranium grandiflorum Johnson's Blue (hardy geranium) 78
Gerbera daisy 30, 110
Giant hogweed (*Heracleum sibiricum*) 86
Gladioli 92
Globe thistle (*Echinops ritro*) 84
    Golden Heart (dahlia) 100
Gourds (*Curcubitaceae*) 122
    Granat (Astilbe) 72
Grapes 50, 124
Grape hyacinth (Muscari) 30, 36, 42, 44, 48, 52
Grass, esparto (*Stipa tenaciosima*) 24
Grass, feather (*Stipa pennata*) 24

Grass, Yorkshire fog (*Holcus lanatus* and *albo-variegatus*) 40, 76, 78, 114, 116, 138
Greuze (tulip) 40
Ground elder (*Aegopodium podagraria*) 86
Guelder rose (*Viburnum opulus*) 40, 48, 94, 106
Guernsey lily (Nerine) 116, 118

Haemanthus katherinae (red Cape lily) 90
Happy End (Gladiolus) 92
Harmony (lily) 46, 68
Hawthorn (*Craetaegus oxycantha*) 64
Hawthorn (*Craetaegus monogyna*) 66
Hawthorn berries 106
Hazard (dahlia) 100
Hazel (*Corylus avellana contorta tourtosa*) 26
Hazel, winter (*Corylopsis spicata*) 44, 76
Heather (*Erica*) 98, 108
Heather (*Erica arborea*) 66
Heather (*Erica carnea*) 52, 66, 108
Heather (*Erica gracilis*) 26
Heather (*Erica mediterranea*) 52, 66, 108
Heather (*Erica tetralix*) 108
Hedera (ivy) 24, 30, 36, 42, 70, 112, 120
Helenium (*Helenium pumilum aurantiacum*) 82
Helianthus 94
Helianthus annuus 94
Helianthus annuus intermedius 94
Helianthus cucumerifolius stella 94
Helianthus nanus, Golden Globe 94
Helichrysum bracteatum (everlasting flower) 24
Helichrysum bracteatum monstrosum plenum (everlasting flower) 24, 138, 140
Helleborus caucasicus purpureus (lenten rose) 124
Hemlock, speckled (*Conium maculatum*) 86
Hemp-agrimony (*Eupatorium cannabinum*) 86
Heracleum (hogsweed) 74, 86, 114
Heracleum sibiricum (giant hogsweed) 86, 100
Hibiscus 76
Hippophae rhamnoides (sea buckthorn) 106
Hochsommer (gladiolus) 92
Hogsweed (Heracleum) 74, 86, 114
Holcus lanatus (Yorkshire fog grass) 40, 76, 78, 114, 116, 138
Holcus lanatus albo-variegatus 40, 76, 114, 116

Holly (*Ilex aquifolium*) 18, 24, 30, 126, 128, 130, 132, 134
Holly, variegated (*Ilex aquifolium argentea-marginata*) 128
Holly, variegated (*Ilex aquifolium aureo-marginata*) 128, 130
Holm oak (*Quercus ilex*) 140
Honesty seed pods (*Lunaria annua*) 140
Horse chestnut (Aesculus) 56
Horseradish (*Cochlearia armorica*) 74
Hosta fortunei 114
Haycinth 12, 32, 46, 48, 52, 66
Hydrangea hortensia 50, 64, 66, 104
Hydrangea paniculata grandiflora 104, 108

Iceland moss (*Cetraria islandica*) 18, 50, 128, 130, 132
Ilex aquifolium (holly) 128, 132
Ilex aquifolium argentea-marginata 128
Ilex aquifolium aureo-marginata 128, 130
Incense cedar (*Libroceorus decurrens*) 136
Iris 18, 38, 42, 48, 78
Iris hollandica (Dutch iris) 46, 50, 52, 64, 84
Iris pseudocaris 114
Iris reticulata 42
Ivy, variegated (Hedera) 24, 30, 36, 42, 70, 112, 120

Japanese azaleas (*Rhododendron obtusa*) 34
Japanese cedar (*Cryptomeria japonica*) 136
Japanese cherry (*Prunus Kanzan, Prunus Amanogawa*) 56, 66
Japanese hazel (*Hammamelis japonica*) 30
Japanese larch (*Larix leptolepsis*) 136
Jonquil 38
Juniper 76, 114
Juniperus chinensis 136

Knapweed (*Centaurea calcitrapa*) 74, 80
Knapweed (*Centaurea jacea*) 74, 80
Knapweed (*Centaurea rhenana*) 74, 80

Koikwitzia amabilis 76

Lady's mantle (Alchemilla) 60
Lamb's ear (*Stachys lanata*) 88
Lamium purpureum (Deadnettle) 44
　Lampe (pompom dahlia) 102
Larch (*Larix decidua*) 136
Larix decidua (Larch) 136
Larix leptolepsis (Japanese larch) 136
Larkspur (*Delphinium ajacis*) 78, 138
Lemon 44, 48
Lenten rose (*Helleborus caucasicus purpureus*) 124
Liatris 104
Librocedrus decurrens (incense cedar) 136
Lilac (*Syringa vulgaris*) 9, 40, 48, 52, 66, 126
Lily 46, 68, 112, 116
Lily-flowered tulip 50
Lily-of-the-valley (*Convallaria majalis*) 42, 62, 114
　Long island (Gladiolus) 92
Lonicera 76
Love-in-a-mist (*Nigella damascena*) 138
Love-lies-bleeding (*Amaranthus caudatus*) 72
Lychnis flos-cuculi (ragged robin) 86

Magnolia amabilis 76
Mahonia aquifolium 52, 56, 124
Malus varieties (crab apple) 11, 26, 54, 106, 110, 112
Maranta tricolor 116
Marguerite (*Chrysanthemum maximum*) 50, 78
Marguerite, wild 86
Marsh hog's fennel (*Peucadanum palustre*) 86, 100
Marsh-marigold (*Caltha palustris*) 114
Mespilus, the snowy (*Amelanchier canadensis*) 92
Mespilus (*Amelanchier spicata*) 92
Michaelmas daisy (Aster) 108
Milfoil (*Achillea* Perry's white) 78. 88
Mimosa (*Acacia dealbata*) 21, 30, 32
Monarda didyma Mahogany (bergamot) 78
Monkshood (*Aconitum napellus*) 78, 140
　Moorplace (pompom dahlia) 102
　Mount Hood (daffodil) 38
　Mrs. R. O. Backhouse (daffodil) 38

Muscari (grape hyacinth) 30, 36, 42, 44, 48, 52
Muscari armeniacum 42
Mushroom 48
　Music Hall (daffodil) 38
Myosotis hybrida (forget-me-not) 9, 54
Myrica gale (bog myrtle) 32
Myrrhis odorata (sweet cicely) 86

Narcissus 20, 24, 32, 38, 46, 54, 68
Narcissus odorus plenus 38
Narcissus Poetaz 38
Narcissus Trevithian 38, 52
Narcissus triandus 38
Nephrolepsis (fern) 40
Nerine sarniensis (Guernsey lily) 116, 118
　New Dawn (rose) 80
Nigella damascena (love-in-a-mist) 138
Nypa fruticans (palm) 140

Oak branches 90
Oak leaves 100
Oats 78
Onion 68
Onopordon acanthium (thistle) 84
Onopordon arabicum 84
Opium poppy (*Papaver somniferum*) 136
　Orange Giant (gladiolus) 92
　Orange Queen (narcissus) 38
Orchid 120
Oriental hawthorn (*Crataegus orientalis*) 106
Oriental poppy 18, 21
Ornamental grass (*Agrostis tenuis*) 78
Ornamental grass (*Briza media*) 78
Ornamental grass (*Holcus lanatus*) 40, 78, 114, 116, 138
Ornamental grass (*Holcus lanatus albo-variegatus*) 40, 76, 114, 116
Ornamental grass (*Stenotaphrum*) 40
Ornamental grass (*Stipa pennata*) 24
Ornamental grass (*Stipa tenaciosima*) 24
　Ostara (hyacinth) 48, 52

Palm (*Chamaerops*) 130, 132
Palm (*Nypa fruticans*) 140
Papaver somniferum (opium poppy) 136
Paperwhite narcissus 12
Parsnip, large water (*Sium latifolium*) 86
Pasque flower (*Anemone pulsatilla*) 140
Passiflora coerulea (passion flower) 108
Passion flower (*Passiflora coerulea*) 108
   Peace (rose) 92
Peach (*Prunus persica*) 56, 66
Pear 11, 106
   Peerless Pink (tulip) 70
Peppers (*Capsicum*) 68, 134
Pernettya mucronata 108, 110, 122, 124
Peucadanum palustre (marsh hog's fennel) 86, 100
Phoenix dactylifera (date palm) 132, 134
Physalis franchetti (Chinese lantern plant) 122, 140
   Picardie (gladiolus) 92
Picea abies (common spruce) 130, 134
Picea amorica (Serbian spruce) 130
Picea pungens (blue spruce) 130, 132, 134
Picea pungens (Colorado spruce) 124
Pieris floribunda (andromeda) 44
   Pilgrim (tulip) 40
Pimpinella saxifraga (saxifrage) 86
   Pink pearl (rhododendron) 58
Poinsettia (*Euphorbia pulcherrima*) 21
Polianthes tuberose 88
Polyanthus 32
Pompom dahlias 102, 112
Poppy, oriental 7, 18, 21
Poppy, wild 18, 21, 24, 78, 86
Portuguese grass (*Stenotaphrum*) 40
Potentilla 76
   Preludium (tulip) 28, 70
Primrose 32
   Princess Irene (tulip) 68
   Princess Marijke (rhododendron) 58
   Prosperity (lily) 68
Protea grandiflora 140
Protea mellifera 140
Protea species 140
Prunes 50
Prunus 11, 46, 56
Prunus amanogawa (Japanese cherry) 56, 66
Prunus amygdalus (almond) 46, 56, 66
Prunus armeniaca (apricot) 56, 66

Prunus avium (cherry) 56, 66
Prunus kanzan (Japanese cherry) 56, 66
Prunus padus (bird cherry) 92
Prunus persica (peach) 56, 66
Prunus triloba plena (dwarf almond) 56, 66
Pseudotsuga douglassii (Douglas fir) 136
Purple black common elder (*Sambus nigra*) 94
   Purple star (tulip) 40
   Purpureum (*Acrolineum roseum*) 138
Pussy-willow (*Salix acutifolia*) 46
Pyracantha coccinea (firethorn) 106, 112

Queen of the night (tulip) 58
Quince (*Chaenomeles Japonica*) 26, 120, 122
Quince (*Cydonia oblonga*) 120

Radishes 50
Ragged robin (*Lychnis flos-cuculi*) 12, 86
Ranunculus acer (buttercup) 12, 62, 64, 86
Red mountain elder (*Sambus racemosa*) 94, 106
   Renaissance (dahlia) 100
Rhododendron 58
Rhododendron gandavense (Ghent azalea) 66
Rhododendron Japonicum or *Molle* (*Azalea mollis*) 58
Rhododendron leaves 90
Rhododendron obtusa (Japanese azalea) 34
Rhododendron ponticum 66
Roses, 18, 20, 21, 24, 42, 60, 66, 70, 72, 76, 80, 82, 88, 96, 98, 104, 106, 108, 118, 124, 132, 134
   Rosy Gem (*Acrolineum roseum*) 138
Rowan berry (*Sorbus Aucuparia*) 106
Rudbeckia purpurea 72
Rumex acetosa (sorrel) 90
Rushes (*Butomus umbellatus*) 86

Saintpaulia (African violet) 48, 54, 76, 84, 90, 120
Salix acutifolia (pussy willow) 46
Sambucus nigra (common elder) 94, 106
Sambucus racemosa (red mountain elder) 94
Saxifrage (*Pimpinella saxifraga*) 86
Scabious (*Scabiosa caucasia*) 84, 90

Scarlet plume (*Euphorbia fulgens*) 126
Scilla 12
Sea buckthorn (*Hippophae rhamnoides*) 106
Sea holly (*Eryngium hybridum*) 84
Seed umbrellas 106
Semi-cactus dahlia 100
Service tree (*Sorbus torminalis*) 106
Siderita candidans (Everlasting flower) 88
   Silver chimes (Narcissus) 38
   Silver rose (*Acrolineum roseum*) 138
Sium latifolium (large water parsnip) 86
   Smiling queen (tulip) 28, 70
Snapdragon (*Antirrhinum majus grandiflorus*) 64, 80
Snowberry (*Symphoricarpus*) 108, 110
Snowdrop (*Galanthus nivalis*) 9, 12, 36, 42
Solanum, tropical 130
   Sonora (rose) 92
Sorbus aucuparia (rowan) 106
Sorbus torminalis (service tree) 106
Sorrel (*Rumex acetosa*) 90
Sphagnum 16, 18, 24, 30 etc.
Spider orchid (*Arachnis moschifera*) 120
Spider plant (*Chorophytum comosum*) 40
Spindle tree (*Euonymus europaeus*) 106
Spiraea 106
Spruce, blue (*Picea pungens*) 130, 132, 134
Spruce, Colorado (*Picea pungens*) 124
Spruce, common (*Picea abies*) 130, 134
Spruce, Serbian (*Picea armorica*) 130
Stachys lanata (lamb's ears) 88
Star thistle (*Centaurea calcitrapa*) 80
Statice (*Statice sinuata*) 138
Statice, perennial (*Limonium tataricum*) 138
Stenotaphrum (Portuguese grass) 40
   Sterling Silver (rose) 104
Stipa pennata (feather grass) 24
Stipa tenaciosima (esparto grass) 24
Sunflower 94, 100, 114
Swamp cypress (*Taxodium distichum*) 136
Sweet flag (*Acorus calamus*) 114
Sweet peas 12, 18
Sweet-william (*Dianthus barbatus*) 28, 138
Symphoricarpus (Snowberry) 108, 110
Syringa vulgaris (lilac) 40, 48, 52, 66, 126

Tagetes erecta flore plena (African marigold) 18, 82

Tanacetum vulgare (tansy) 86
Tansy (*Tanacetum vulgare*) 86
Taxodium distichum (swamp cypress) 136
Taxus baccata semperaurea (golden yew) 34
Teasel (*Dipsacus*) 84, 140
Thistle (*Onopordon*) 74, 84
Thistle (*Onopordon acanthium*) 84
Thistle, carline (*Carlina vulgaris*) 140
Thistle, sea (*Eryngium campestre*) 140
Thistle, silver (*Carlina acaulis*) 140
Thistle, woolly (*Cirsium eriophorum*) 140
Thuja occ. woodwardi 34, 76
Toadstools 12
Tomato 68
Traveller's joy (*Clematis vitalba*) 118
Trollius 50
Tuberose (*Polyanthes tuberose*) 88
Tulip seeds 120, 136
Tulips, 9, 12, 18, 20, 28, 32, 40, 46, 50, 58, 64, 66, 68, 70

Umbelliferous plants 86, 100
Umbrella plant 70

Vaccinium corymbosum (bilberry) 106
   Van der Neer (tulip) 40
Veronica incana 64
Veronica spicata 74
Viburnum opulus sterile (guelder rose) 40, 58, 94, 106
Violet 12

Walnuts 50, 130
Water parsnip, large (*Sium latifolium*) 100
Water plantain (*Alisma plantago aquatica*) 114
Wheat 78
   White Dorothy Perkins (rose) 88
Willow herb (*Epilobium augustifolium*) 86
Witch hazel (*Hamamelis mollis*) 30
Witch hazel catkins 9

Yellow flag (*Iris pseudocaris*) 114
Yellow peppers (*Capsicum annuum*) 134
Yew, golden (*Taxus baccata semperaurea*) 34
Yorkshire fog (grass) 40, 76, 78, 114, 116, 138
Yuka (Ornamental cabbage) 116

Zantedeschia (Arum) 114
Zantedeschia albi-maculata 114
Zinnias 20

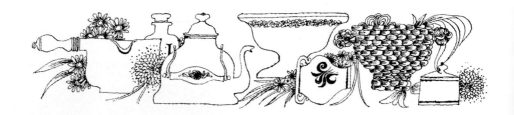